Reasoning and Writing

A Direct Instruction Program

Level C
Teacher's Guide

Siegfried Engelmann

Jerry Silbert

A Division of The McGraw·Hill Companies

Columbus, Ohio

Cover Credits

(t) ©SuperStock, (b) Animal Graphics.

SRA/McGraw-Hill

A Division of The **McGraw·Hill** *Companies*

Contents

Program Summary

Facts about *Reasoning and Writing, Level C*

Students who are appropriately placed in Level C	Students who have completed Level B or who pass the placement criteria for Level C

Placement criteria	Students are able to read on at least a second-grade level
	Students meet placement test criteria for:
	  Following instructions
	  Copying words at the rate of 10 words per minute
	  Spelling copied words correctly
	(See the placement test on page 13.)

Format of lessons	Scripted presentations for all activities Program designed for presentation to entire class
Number of lessons	110 total (including 10 test lessons)
Scheduled time for Language periods	40 minutes per period Usually, one lesson can be completed in each period
Weekly schedule	3-4 lessons per week
Teacher's material	Teacher's Guide Presentation Book Answer Key Booklet
Student's material	Textbook Workbook
In-program tests	Every 10th lesson
Remedies	Specified as part of each test lesson
Additional material	Writing Extensions, Grade 3 Teacher's Presentation and blackline masters for extensions lessons 1–90

Scope and Sequence for *Reasoning and Writing, Level C*

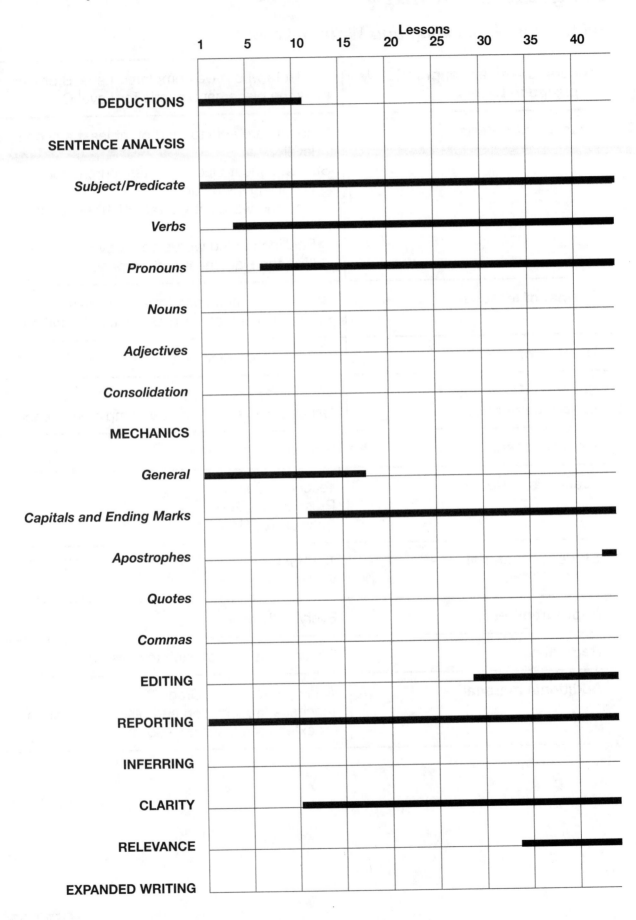

Lessons

| | 1 | 5 | 10 | 15 | 20 | 25 | 30 | 35 | 40 |

DEDUCTIONS

SENTENCE ANALYSIS

Subject/Predicate

Verbs

Pronouns

Nouns

Adjectives

Consolidation

MECHANICS

General

Capitals and Ending Marks

Apostrophes

Quotes

Commas

EDITING

REPORTING

INFERRING

CLARITY

RELEVANCE

EXPANDED WRITING

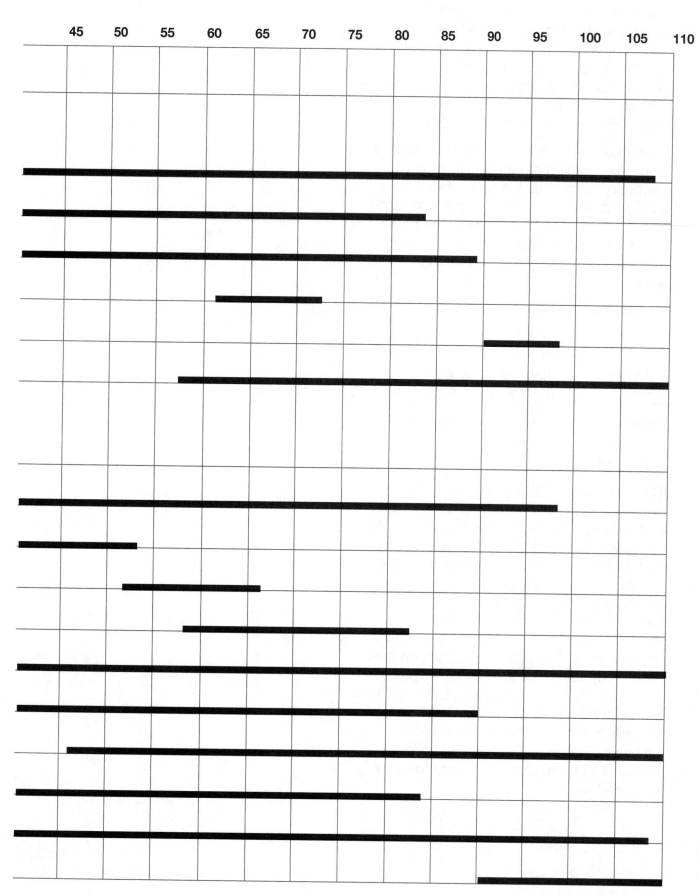

Scheduling

There are different scheduling options to cover the 110 lessons of Level C in a school year. The simplest option is to present the program three days a week, starting in September. If the program is scheduled on Mondays, Wednesdays and Fridays, you will have sufficient time to mark papers.

If the class has a relatively high percentage of low-performing students, you may use the option of scheduling four lessons a week and using only three of them to teach new lessons. The fourth scheduled period is a "catch up" lesson during which you work only with the lower-performing students.

A third option is to follow this schedule:

	Sept.–Jan.	Feb.–end of year
Scheduled periods	5 days per week	3 days per week
Projected lessons per week	4 lessons per week	2 lessons per week

The advantage of this option is that it permits you to provide relatively more time on the longer passages that students write near the end of the program. During the first 70 lessons (which would be presented before the end of January), students write relatively short passages. During the latter part of the program (lessons 71–110), students work on more extensive assignments. They need feedback on their work. The feedback is more easily provided if you plan to teach only two lessons a week but schedule three periods in which to achieve this goal. The additional period can be used to provide feedback and allow students to listen to and respond to other students' work.

How the Program Is Different

Reasoning and Writing C teaches basic writing skills and the reasoning that is required to apply these skills to writing assignments that are manageable for the students. The program differs from traditional approaches to introducing writing in the following ways:

Field Tested

Reasoning and Writing **has been shaped through extensive field testing and revising based on problems students and teachers encountered.** This work was completed before the program was published. The development philosophy of *Reasoning and Writing* is that, if teachers or students have trouble with material presented, the program is at fault. Revisions are made to correct the problems.

Organization

The organization of how skills are introduced, developed and reviewed is unique. In traditional programs, the curriculum is called a spiral, which means that students work exclusively on a particular topic for a few lessons. Then a new topic (often unrelated to the preceding topic) is presented. *Reasoning and Writing* does not follow this format for the following reasons:

a) During a period, it is not productive to work only on a single topic. If new information is being presented, it is very easy for students to become overwhelmed with the information. A more sensible procedure, and one that has been demonstrated to be superior in studies of learning and memory, is to distribute the practice, so that, instead of working 45 minutes on a single topic, students work each day for possibly 10 minutes on each of four topics.

b) When full-period topics are presented, it becomes very difficult for the teacher to provide practice on the latest skills that had been taught. Unless the skills that had been taught are used and reviewed, student performance will deteriorate, and the skills will have to be retaught when they again appear. A more sensible organization is to present work on skills continuously (not discontinuously), so that students work on a particular topic (such as pronoun clarity) for part of 20 or 30 lessons, not for 5 or 6 entire lessons at a time. In this context of continuous development of skills, review becomes automatic, and reteaching becomes unnecessary because students use the skills on almost every lesson.

c) When skills are not developed continuously, students must learn a lot of new concepts during a short period and are also expected to become "automatic" in applying the new concepts and skills. For most students, adequate learning will not occur. A more sensible way is to develop skills and concepts in small steps, so that students are not required to learn as much new material at a time, which means they receive a sufficient amount of practice to become facile or automatic in applying what they learn.

d) When skills are not developed continuously, students and teachers may develop very negative attitudes about mastery. Students often learn that they are not expected to "learn" the new material because it will go away in a few days. Teachers become frustrated because they often understand that students need a lot more practice, but they are unable to provide it and at the same time move through the program at a reasonable rate. Again, the continuous development of skills solves this problem because students learn very quickly that what is presented is used in this lesson, in the next lesson, and so forth. When the practice is sufficient, students develop the set or expectation needed for learning a skill to mastery because it is something they will need in the immediate future.

e) When lessons are not clearly related to "periods" of time, the teacher has no precise way to gauge the performance of the students or to judge how long to spend on a particular "lesson." A more reasonable procedure is to organize material into lessons, each requiring so much time to teach. The teacher then knows that the lesson has the potential of teaching students within a class period of 45 minutes.

f) The focus of *Reasoning and Writing* is on writing; however, students need various skills to write acceptably. These skills are taught in isolation (or in a simple form that provides students with lots of practice) and are then funneled into more complex applications. The skills that are taught are organized in *tracks*. A track is an ongoing development of a particular topic. Within each lesson, work from 3 to 5 tracks is presented. The teaching presentations are designed so it is possible to present the entire lesson in 45 minutes (although some lessons may be shorter and others may require more time for lower performers).

From lesson to lesson, the work on new skills develops a small step at a time so that students are not overwhelmed with new information and receive enough practice both to master skills and to become facile with them. Students, therefore, learn quickly about *learning new concepts* and realize that what they are learning has utility because they will use it.

Focus on Writing

The first levels of *Reasoning and Writing* (Levels A and B) focused primarily on higher-order thinking skills that serve students in understanding the "ideas" that are expressed in stories and accounts. The focus of Level C is on writing. The transition to writing is a relatively big step because it involves many skills that are unique. The diagram below presents an overview of the various skills that a writer needs to write effectively.

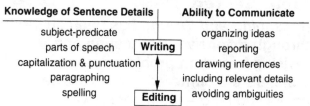

The left side of the diagram consists of mechanical skills, spelling, punctuation and knowledge of sentence structure. These skills are not trivial.

Third-grade students typically have trouble reading what they have written. (They often don't read exactly what they've written, but rather what they think they've written.)

The third-grader often writes very slowly—possibly no more than 10–12 words per minute. Writing at this rate is an impediment to holding onto ideas long enough to express them in sentences.

The third-grader typically does not spell accurately and is not familiar with basic punctuation or capitalization rules.

Grammar is related to punctuation. How does the writer know where to place periods and commas? If the writer writes a regular-order simple sentence that begins with a subject and ends with a predicate, no commas are needed. The period goes at the end of the sentence. However, if parts are missing, parts are inverted, or the sentence includes parts that are not intended for the regular-order sentence (such as direct quotes), punctuation is needed. The writer should have knowledge of basic sentence structure and knowledge of how the structure relates to punctuation and how it affects communicating with the reader.

The left side of the diagram, therefore, suggests much that should be taught before the student is able to perform even basic writing assignments in a way that will lead to success. The problem is that students who receive voluminous feedback on mechanical mistakes typically are not able to process the information in a way that will lead to positive changes in their writing. The feedback simply confirms to them that they aren't doing very well. So the skills should be taught in a manner that does not overwhelm the student.

The right side of the diagram involves communicating, which is the application of thinking skills. The basic rules of organizing a passage or story are based on the idea that the reader doesn't share the writer's understanding. If the writer's impressions are to be shared as intended, they must be organized in a way that communicates. The writer should not omit details that are necessary for the reader to see the links that the writer is trying to express.

Organization is closely related to clarity. Clarity of pronouns is something that third-graders may not understand well. Students who have gone though Level B of *Reasoning and Writing* should have a good understanding of clarity. However, being able to identify unclear pronoun referents in someone else's writing is usually a lot easier than identifying it in your own writing.

Finally, the passage should contain only information that is relevant to the topic or theme of the passage.

All categories on the right side of the diagram suggest thinking and analytical skills that must be taught to the student.

The Process of Writing

Much has been written about the idea that "writing is a process," a notion that is sound in several fundamental ways. The first is that you don't try to write and edit lavishly at the same time. Instead, you first write and then edit. What "writing as a process" does not convey is the host of skills that must be orchestrated if the students are to learn quickly. Certainly it is possible to permit students to write a passage that is subsequently edited, reedited, and finally "published." The question is: Who did the significant editing and rewriting? Let's say that you tore up the final product and told the student, "That's how to do it; now it's your turn. Write the same thing and see if you can end up with a story as good as the one I just tore up." Would the student now be able to do it, or would the student still be dependent on you or someone else to correct mistakes after the fact?

Level C teaches writing as a process, but one that involves the integration of **skills** that are pretaught, with initial writing assignments that are relatively simple and that require only basic sentences, which students are able to write. Progressive changes in writing assignments incorporate new skills that are taught in the program.

Level C is based on these criteria of effective instructional sequences:

1. The work seems relatively easy because the students succeed.
2. The skill introduction is "cumulative," which means that, when a new skill is taught, it is practiced extensively for the remainder of the program.
3. All skills that students need for various applications are pretaught.
4. The errors students make can be easily corrected by the teacher.

The ultimate test of a well-designed program is the teacher's ability to correct students' mistakes. If the teacher can correct all mistakes by referring to something that students have been taught, the program is well designed. In a well-designed program, the teaching always comes first, and the applications follow. The teacher is always able to correct mistakes that students make on assignments that require them to use what they have learned. In contrast, the poorly designed program makes corrections very difficult because the preteaching is inadequate.

Global Strategies

Level C organizes skills so they are related to what the students already know and to what they are taught in Level C. The following descriptions provide a global view of how these relationships are created.

SUBJECT-PREDICATE, GRAMMAR, PUNCTUATION

Although grammar is currently downplayed (primarily because traditional attempts to teach it often fail), grammar is not difficult for students if it is related to sentences. There are two principle reasons for teaching grammar:

1. The understanding of basic grammar provides a communication link between teacher and student.
2. Dictionaries categorize words according to their parts of speech. For students to use a dictionary productively, they should understand how the different meanings relate to the parts of speech.

Grammar relates to simple declarative sentences:

He went to the store.

The first part of the sentence names. That part is the **subject** (He). The second part of the sentence tells more about the subject (went to the store.) That's the **predicate.**

All declarative sentences must have both parts—subject and predicate. As long as the sentence begins with the subject and no parts are missing, no special punctuation is needed—simply a period at the end. This rule also holds for sentences that are longer:

Tom and Mary went to the store after Mrs. Jones came home.

If the order of the parts is changed, however, punctuation is needed:

After Mrs. Jones came home, Tom and Mary went to the store.

The sentence has the same set of words as the original, but it has been transformed to begin with part of the predicate. The comma simply marks where the subject begins.

Other punctuation rules have to do with missing parts, such as a missing *and.* In this sentence, no special punctuation is needed:

They slid down the hill and rolled over and started to laugh.

In this sentence, punctuation is needed because part of the sentence is missing—the word *and:*

They slid down the hill, rolled over and started to laugh.

Parts of speech are related to the position of words in the sentence. The subject must either contain a noun or be a pronoun. Even sentences that are strange follow this rule:

Running is a lot of fun.

The sentence names running, so that's the **subject.** Since the subject must be a pronoun or must contain a noun, the subject must be some kind of noun.

The first part of the predicate is usually a verb. (Exceptions are usually interruptions created by adverbs, such as: He **usually** works all afternoon.) The verb may contain one word or more than one word. Again, the relationships are best shown through transformations. The regular-order sentence is the starting point:

She <u>went</u> to the store. She <u>was going</u> to the store.

Went and *was going* serve exactly the same function; therefore, they must be the same part of speech.

For basic sentences, nouns are the names that occur in subjects.

<u>Her little puppy</u> had lots of fleas.

The last word is *puppy*—the last word in the subject is usually a noun.

The advantage of relating nouns to subjects with more than one word is that it provides the learner with a test of what's a noun and what isn't. Nouns are free-floating elements that can occur in the predicate as well as in the subject. A test of words is to see how they would work as the last word of the subject. Those that "make sense" are nouns. Often verbal descriptions of what is a noun are not particularly enlightening: Nouns name persons, places, or things. However, if the student has a method of testing words to determine whether they are nouns, the ideas expressed by the descriptions are a lot easier to learn.

The words that precede the noun in the subject are **adjectives.** It is possible to classify some of them as a type of adjective:

A little puppy had fleas.

The word *A* can be classified as an article. However, it's also an adjective. Any word that precedes a noun and tells about the noun is an adjective. That rule provides a test for adjectives that occur in the predicate:

He fed the little puppy.

Puppy is a noun. *The* and *little* precede *puppy* and tell about *puppy*. Therefore, they are adjectives.

All the relationships described above are taught in Level C. Grammar is treated as a position game, because that's what it is. Unless students understand grammar as such, they'll have a lot of trouble understanding why *losing* is a verb in this sentence:

Our team was losing.

and why it is an adjective in this sentence:

The losing player received a silver medal.

and why it is a noun in this sentence:

Losing is not fun.

Grammar is closely related to punctuation, because a major reason for punctuation is to indicate that the regular-order nature of the sentence has been violated. It can be violated by inversions of parts:

Shortly before the sun rose, Ruffy growled.

(Part of the predicate appears before the subject.)

Another violation is on nonrestrictive parts. Nonrestrictive parts are set off from the rest of the sentence because they function as asides:

Of course, he was tired.

Direct quotes require lots of punctuation because they are elements not intended for regular-order sentences:

He said, "I am tired."

(In the parallel sentence: *He said that he was tired,* no special punctuation is needed.)

COMMUNICATION DETAILS

The ability to communicate in writing involves a host of higher-order thinking skills. For the simplest writing assignment, the student names the character in a picture and tells the main thing the character did. This assignment implies that the student is able to discriminate between "reporting" and "not reporting," and between "the main thing the character did" and some ancillary action.

For some writing assignments, the student must infer what must have happened in a picture sequence before writing an account that includes all the relevant information. These assignments assume that the student is able to identify details and is able to express them in sentences.

The student must organize ideas so they present a clear picture to the reader. Clarity means that the writer "sets the scene," introduces characters carefully and describes events in a way that avoids ambiguity. Again, the ability to write "clearly" implies that the student understands the difference between passages that are not clear and those that are, between passages that are well organized and those that aren't.

Level C provides teaching in all the component skills the student needs to organize and write basic passages.

REPORTING

Initial writing assignments require students to report. Students learn to discriminate between sentences that "report" and those that don't report. Students are presented with a picture and a series of statements, some of which report on what the picture shows and others that don't.

Part A

Circle **reports** if a sentence reports on what the picture shows.
Circle **does not report** if the sentence does not report on what the picture shows.

1. The three men were brothers.	reports	does not report
2. Three men fished from a boat.	reports	does not report
3. The men were going to have fish for dinner.	reports	does not report
4. A big dog stood in the boat.	reports	does not report
5. All the men wore hats.	reports	does not report
6. One man held a net.	reports	does not report
7. One fishing pole bent down toward the water.	reports	does not report
8. A large fish was on the end of the line.	reports	does not report

Students report on what pictures show. Students are not permitted to "make up" scenarios about what happened. Students describe what the characters did. They do not tell what the characters were thinking or feeling, or why they did what they did.

Level C restricts initial writing assignments to "reporting" for several reasons:

a) Students of varying abilities will tend to write the same set of sentences if they are required to report. However, if students are permitted to write whatever their imagination dictates, great variation will occur. Although some of the students will write clever passages, these passages don't serve as good models to the other students because they are the product of many skills that have not been taught to the other students. Also, the lines between acceptable and unacceptable passages will not be clear to many students because the passage they write may be quite different from those other students created. In this context, students find it difficult to figure out what's acceptable and what isn't. In summary, when the assignment is restricted to "reporting," the criteria for an acceptable passage are clear, the variability from student to student is reduced, and all students are able to succeed because the assignment does not involve skills that have not been taught in the program. The goal is not to teach a few students well, but to teach all of them well.

b) To write effectively, the student must learn to operate under various constraints. Not all writing follows the same form; not all addresses the same reader. Ultimately, students will have to learn to "check" their passages for a large number of criteria. Writing that is limited to reporting is a good constraint for beginners.

c) The tests of reporting are relatively simple. Basically, if students cannot find details of a picture that correspond to what they wrote, they haven't reported.

d) Finally, reporting sets the stage for "inferring," which is taught later. If students understand what it is to report, they can appreciate the difference between reporting and inferring, which involves interpretations based on a picture sequence but not shown by the sequence.

Later in Level C, students learn to draw inferences. The primary teaching occurs through picture sequences that show events.

bucket   fell   burn

The middle picture is missing, which signals that the student must draw inferences about what must have happened in the middle picture. The procedure they follow is to use picture details as **evidence** of what must have happened. They do this by comparing the first picture and the last. Any differences between details of these pictures signals an inference. For instance, the candles in the first and last pictures are not in the same place. Therefore, something must have happened to the candle in the middle picture. The woman is not doing the same thing in the first and last picture; therefore, she must have done something in the middle picture. By comparing other details of the two pictures (such as the newspaper), the students gather specific information for creating **minimal** statements about what must have happened. Note that students are not to make up a great yarn about what happened, but are to use the information about differences between the pictures to identify the minimal things that must have happened. For example:

The candle fell on the newspapers. The newspapers started to burn.

Once students have learned the basic "game" for creating inferences, they perform on assignments that permit more latitude in how they fill in the missing details.

CLARITY

Level C teaches students the basic rules about clarity. In addition to the sentence format of first naming someone and then telling the main thing the person did, students are introduced to activities that focus on the idea that what somebody writes may be perfectly clear to the writer but not to the reader.

a) Initial exercises in clarity present pictures and a group of sentences.

Part E | Read each sentence. Write the letter of each picture that shows what the sentence says.

1. Brett ate fruit.
2. A person ate fruit.
3. Sandra ate an apple.
4. A person ate a banana.

Students identify the pictures each sentence could tell about. One sentence tells about only one picture. That is the preferable sentence, and that is the basic game of clarity—to describe so that the reader is able to visualize the details that are described by the passage in a way that creates very little ambiguity.

b) Students work with passages that "tell about" a picture, but that use unclear words. When the words are unclear, the passage could tell about any number of pictures. For instance, students are presented with a picture that shows a young girl, dressed in a cowgirl outfit, carrying a wooden basket containing a large, striped snake.

The passage:

An animal fell out of a large, old tree. It landed on the soft ground. A person picked it up. The person put it in a container and took it home.

All the sentences have parts that are vague. Students identify the vague words and replace them with more precise descriptions.

c) Students work with passages that have unclear pronouns and apply the rule that, if they are writing about more than one male or more than one female, sentences that use the words *he* or *she* may be unclear. For example:

Ann and Kim were swimming. She wore a bathing cap.

Students refer to a picture in which the girls are labeled and correct the second sentence to make it clear.

d) Students also learn "extended clarity" skills, such as setting a scene. Again, they work from pictures sequences. They examine the details of the first picture and write about those details that would give the reader a clear picture of the story's starting point.

ORGANIZATION

Students are introduced to different organization schemes. The simplest organization involves writing more than one sentence about a picture. The first sentence tells the main thing the person did. The following sentences provide details. These exercises **teach** main idea and supporting detail in the appropriate context—writing. The tasks are relatively easy because students have already been taught the skills needed to write "main idea" sentences for pictures. Students simply tell the main thing the person did.

After students have worked on simple assignments, they are presented with pictures that show groups of individuals. For example, a picture may show a group of children cleaning a room. No two children are doing the same thing, but all are engaged in the "main" activity of cleaning the room. Students start with the statement about what the group did; then they write about the individuals and tell what each of them did.

More complicated organizations are presented as students learn to write direct quotes (to tell what different characters said), to set the scene for longer passages and to work from written descriptions.

EDITING

Editing activities are presented throughout Level C. Their purpose is to reinforce the various communication skills and mechanical skills taught in the program. They are coordinated with the students' writing assignments so that students are not required to apply a particular rule, procedure, or skill until they have edited passages for violations of the rule, procedure or skill. For example, students edit passages for pronoun clarity before they are held accountable for writing passages that have clear pronouns. Students do not write passages with direct quotes until they have edited sentences that are supposed to present direct quotes.

The editing activities are extended to the students' writing through checks for specific aspects of what the students wrote. The rationale for checks is that students should first write and then check their writing for various criteria. This process is easier for students if they understand the various criteria. Checks in Level C are a very important part of the teaching that students receive. The specific checks for a writing assignment appear in the student textbook. Here's an example:

Check 1
Does each sentence begin with a capital and end with a period?

Check 2
Does each sentence tell the main thing?

Check 3
Does each sentence tell what somebody or something **did?**

After students write their stories, they read them for each of the checks. By dealing with the checks one at a time, students receive practice in applying criteria one at a time. Later, as they become more proficient at editing for multiple criteria, they will become more facile both at reading for multiple checks and for writing quickly and doing some checking at the same time.

For students, editing their own work is a difficult process. That's why they first learn particular skills in isolation, then they edit someone else's writing for violations, and finally they edit their own writing for possible violations.

In summary, Level C provides an introduction to writing that teaches students skills, procedures and strategies that will serve them for as long as they write. The emphasis is on clarity of communication, not on intricately decorated sentences. Students learn about subject—predicate. They learn basic mechanical rules and communication techniques. Level C honors the notion that writing is a process, and that students should first write and then edit. Level C, however, has been tempered by facts about the specific mistakes that students make and the amount of practice that they need to reliably apply rules and procedures used by good writers. One basic goal of the program is to assure that students understand the criteria that are used to judge writing. By working on frequent editing activities and checking their own work for relevant criteria, they acquire facility at communicating through writing. The skills the students are to use are developed systematically, first in isolation, then in editing activities, and finally as criteria for the students' writing.

At the end of Level C, students are able to look at the writing process as a communication process that gives the reader a clear picture of what the writer is trying to convey.

Placement

Level C is appropriate for students who read on at least the second-grade level, who can copy words at no less than 10 words a minute, and who can follow basic directions. Students who do not meet these criteria will have trouble performing on many of the activities presented in Level C.

A placement test evaluates students' performance at copying and following directions. A reproducible copy of the test appears on page 15. The test is group administered and requires about 10 minutes for students to complete. The script for presenting the test appears below.

Administering the Test

Pass out a test form to each student. Students are to write their name in the space on the top.

Present the following nonscorable (warm up) items and 4 scorable items.

- Get ready to follow some directions. (**Note:** These are nonscorable items.)
- Touch the picture of the dog. (Observe students and give feedback.)
- The dog is not the first or second or third picture. Raise your hand when you know the number for the dog.
- Everybody, what's the number for the dog? (Signal.) 6
  (**Note:** These are scorable items. Allow 5 seconds for each item.)
- I'll tell you directions. Do exactly what the directions tell you to do. Get your pencils ready.
- Listen: Circle the first picture. (Pause 5 seconds.)

- New directions: Make a box around the last picture. (Pause 5 seconds.)
- New directions: Make a line **under** the picture that is just after the bird.
- Listen again: Make a line **under** the picture that is just after the bird. (Pause 5 seconds.)
- New directions: Make a line **over** the picture that is just before the snake.
- Listen again: Make a line over the picture that is just before the snake. (Pause 5 seconds.)
- Everybody, put your pencil down and don't touch it until I tell you.
- Touch the little story that is in the box.
- I'll read that story. Follow along: Three men sat in their boat. One of those men jumped into the water. A big fish chased him.
- Everybody, touch the lines below the story. You're going to copy that whole story. Everybody, touch the letter A. You'll start right after the letter A. You'll copy the story just the way it is written. You'll spell all the words correctly. You'll put in the capital letters and the periods just the way they are shown in the story.
- The first sentence of the story is: Three men sat in their boat. That's the first sentence you'll copy. Then you'll copy the rest of the story. Pencils ready. You have 2 minutes. Get ready. Go. (Time students. After 2 minutes, say:) Everybody, if you're not finished, stop now and put your pencil down.
- (Collect tests.)

Name: _____ Date: _____

Three men sat in their boat. One of those men jumped into the water. A big fish chased him.

A.	

1. Number of errors on picture items	0	**1**	2	3	4		
2. Number of omitted words (words not copied)	0	1	**2**	3	4	5	☐
3. Number of copied words misspelled	0	1	**2**	3	4	5	☐

Scoring the Test

An answer key for the pictures appears below:

On each child's test form, record the number of errors for each criterion.

Line 1: Circle the number of errors the student made on **picture items.** If the child missed no items, circle 0. If the child missed all 4 picture items, circle 4.

Line 2: Circle the number of **omitted words** (words not copied). Read each student's story. Make sure all the sentences have the correct words. Mark any places where the student omitted words. Count the number of omitted words (those overlooked or those at the end of the story that were not written). If the number is 5 or less, circle the appropriate number on line 2. If the number is more than 5, write the number in the box at the end of line 2.

Line 3: Circle the number of **misspelled words.** Mark each misspelled word. Count the number. If the number is 5 or less, circle the appropriate number on line 3. If the number is more than 5, write the number in the box at the end of line 3.

Placement Criteria

Students should not be placed in *Reasoning and Writing, Level C,* unless they meet all the following criteria:

1. The student should read on at least the second-grade level. If you have doubts about the student's reading ability, direct the student to read the following sentences from part A of lesson 1:

1. The three men were brothers.	reports	does not report
2. Three men fished from a boat.	reports	does not report
4. A big dog stood in the boat.	reports	does not report
5. All the men wore hats.	reports	does not report
8. A large fish was on the end of the line.	reports	does not report

Point to each item the student is to read and say: "Read this sentence." If the child gets stuck on a word, tell the word after about 3 seconds. The student should complete the reading in no more than 45 seconds and should make no more than 3 decoding errors. Students who exceed these limits probably do not read well enough to benefit from Level C.

2. The student should pass all the criteria listed on lines 1, 2, and 3 at the bottom of the placement test. The criterion for each line is indicated by the boldfaced number.

1. Number of errors on picture items	0	**1**	2	3	4		
2. Number of omitted words (words not copied)	0	1	**2**	3	4	5	
3. Number of copied words misspelled	0	1	**2**	3	4	5	

If the student's number is to the right of the boldfaced number, the student fails that criterion. If the student makes more than one error on the picture items, the student fails. If the student makes more than two errors on omitted or copied words, the student fails.

If a student passes all the criteria but one and just barely misses meeting that criterion, the student could be placed in Level C.

If more than 20 percent of the class fails to meet the entry criteria for Level C, do not start the program at the beginning of the year. Plan to spend the first two months of school working on basic skills.

FOLLOWING DIRECTIONS

Students who are deficient in following directions should be placed in a program that teaches following directions, (such as *Reasoning and Writing, Level B*).

COPYING RATE AND SPELLING ACCURACY

Students who do not copy fast enough or accurately should practice copying. A good procedure is to devote 15 minutes a day to copying. Write sentences on the chalkboard and direct students to copy them. Try to use sentences they are able to decode.

Set a rate criterion based on 8 words a minute. Award points for students who meet this criterion.

Here's a sample presentation:

- This passage has 32 words. If you copy all the words and spell them correctly in 4 minutes, you earn 4 points. I'll read the passage. Then you'll copy it just as it is written.
- (Read the passage.)
  Pencils ready. Go.
  (Observe students and give positive feedback.)
- Some students are well on their way to earning 4 bonus points. I'm seeing some good, careful copying . . .

When nearly all students can complete the passage in the allotted time (8 words per minute), change the rate to 10 words per minute and award 5 points for completion.

Keep records of student performance. Make a graph that shows class improvement.

Teaching the Program

Level C is designed to be presented to the entire class. You should generally be able to teach one lesson during a 40-minute period. All writing assignments are completed during this period.

Classroom Arrangement

Arrange seating so you can receive very quick information on high performers and low performers. A good plan is to organize the students something like this:

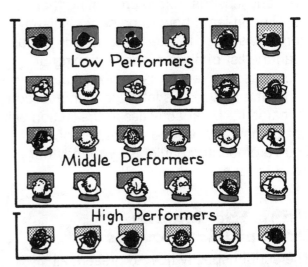

The lowest performers are closest to the front of the classroom. Middle performers are arranged around the lowest performers. Highest performers are arranged around the periphery. With this arrangement, you can position yourself so that, by taking a few steps during the time that students are working, you can sample low, average and high performers.

While different variations of this arrangement are possible, be careful not to seat low performers far from the front-center of the room. The highest performers, understandably, can be farthest from the center because they attend better, learn faster, and need less observation and feedback.

Teaching

When you teach the program, a basic rule is that you should not present from the front of the room. For nearly all activities, you direct work-specified tasks. You should present from somewhere in the middle of the room (in no set place); and as students work, you should move around and quickly observe a good sample of students. Although you won't be able to observe every student working every task, you can observe at least a dozen in a couple of minutes.

Rehearse the lesson before presenting it to the class. Don't simply read the text—act it out. Watch your wording. If you rehearse the early lessons before presenting them, you'll soon learn how to present efficiently from the script. In later lessons, you should scan the list of skills at the beginning of each lesson. New skills are in boldface type. If a new skill is introduced in a lesson, rehearse it. Most activities in the lesson will not be new, but will be a variation of what you've presented earlier, so you may not need to rehearse these activities.

Using the Teacher Presentation Scripts

The scripts specify how to present all activities in a lesson. The first part of the period involves work on skills. The second part on writing.

The script for each lesson indicates precisely how to present each structured activity. The script shows what you say, what you do, and what the student responses should be.

What you say appears in blue type: You say this.

What you do appears in parentheses: (You do this.)

The responses of the students are in italics: *Students say this.*

Follow the specified wording in the script. While wording variations from the specified script are not always dangerous, you will be assured of communicating clearly with the students if you follow the script exactly. The reason is that the wording is controlled, and the tasks are arranged so they provide succinct wording and focus clearly on important aspects of what the students are to do. Although you may at first feel uncomfortable "reading" from a script (and you may feel that the students will not pay attention), follow the scripts very closely; try to present them as if you were saying something important to the students. If you do, you'll find after awhile that working from a script is not difficult and that students indeed respond well to what you say.

A sample script appears on the next page.

1

How you secure
group responses

4. New sentence: A little dog (pause) is running
   down the street. What part names? (Signal.)
   A little dog.
   • New sentence: A boy and a girl (pause) are
     running down the street. What part names?
     (Signal.) *A boy and a girl.*
   • New sentence: Two girls (pause) are eating ice
     cream. What part names? (Signal.) *Two girls.*
   • New sentence: The man and the boy (pause)
     ate ice cream. What part names? (Signal.)
     The man and the boy.
     (Repeat step 4 until firm.)

2

What you firm

5. New sentence: A little rabbit ran under the
   fence. What part names? (Signal.) *A little rabbit.*
   • New sentence: A dog and a cat ran under the
     fence. What part names? (Signal.) *A dog and a
     cat.*
   • New sentence: My brother went to the store.
     What part names? (Signal.) *My brother.*
     (Repeat step 5 until firm.)

3

How you pace
your presentation
to student
performance

6. Everybody, find part B in your workbook. ✔
   Touch each sentence as I read it.
   Sentence 1: Two girls are eating ice cream.
   Sentence 2: A black cat ran under the fence.
   Sentence 3: A man and a woman sat on the
   porch.
   Make a circle around the part of each sentence
   that names. Circle the part that names. Raise
   your hand when you're finished.
   (Observe students and give feedback.)

7. Let's check your work. Make an **X** next to any
   item you missed.
   • Sentence 1: Two girls are eating ice cream.
     Everybody, say the part you circled. (Signal.)
     Two girls.
   • Sentence 2: A black cat ran under the fence.
     Say the part that names. (Signal.) *A black cat.*
   • Sentence 3: A man and a woman sat on the
     porch. Say the part that names. (Signal.)
     A man and a woman.

8. Raise your hand if you got no items wrong. ✔
   Super job.
   • Everyone else, fix up any mistakes you made in
     part B.
     (Observe students and give feedback.)

The arrows show the three different things you'll do that are not spelled out in the script. You'll make sure that group responses involve all the students. You'll also "firm" critical parts of the exercises. And you'll use information based on what the students are doing to judge whether you'll proceed quickly or wait a few more seconds before moving on with the presentation.

ARROW 1: GROUP RESPONSES

Some of the tasks call for group responses. If students respond in unison, you receive good information about whether "most" of the students are performing correctly. The simplest way to signal students to respond together is to adopt a timing practice—just like the timing in a musical piece.

Step 4 presents a task that students respond to in unison.

> New sentence.
> A little dog (pause) is running down the street.
> What part names? (Signal.)
> *A little dog.*

You can signal when students are to respond by nodding, clapping one time, snapping your fingers or tapping your foot. After initially establishing the timing for signals, you can signal through voice inflection only.

Students will not be able to initiate responses together at the appropriate rate unless you follow these rules:

a) Talk first. Pause a standard length of time (possibly 1 second); then signal. Students are to respond on your signal—not after it or before it.

b) Model responses that are paced reasonably. Don't permit students to produce slow, droney responses. These are dangerous because they rob you of the information that can be derived from appropriate group responses. When students respond in a droney way, many

of them are copying responses of others. If students are required to respond at a reasonable speaking rate, all students must initiate responses. Therefore, it's relatively easy to determine which students are not responding and which are saying the wrong thing.

Also, don't permit students to respond at a very fast rate or to "jump" your signal.

To correct mistakes, show students exactly what you want them to do.

> I'm going to answer the right way. My turn to say the answer.
> **A little dog.** Let's see who can answer just that way. Listen:
> A little dog is running down the street. Everybody, what part names? (Signal.)
> *A little dog.*
> Good. You're saying it the right way.

(**Note:** Do not respond with the students unless you are trying to work with them on a difficult response. You present only what's in blue. You do not say the answers with the students, and you should not move your lips or give other spurious clues about what the answer is.)

Think of unison responses this way: If you use them correctly, they provide you with much diagnostic information. They suggest whether you should repeat a task (because the response was weak). They permit you to get information about which students may need more help. They are therefore important early in the program. After students have learned the game, the students will be able to respond on cue with no signal. That will happen, however, only if you always keep a constant time interval between the completion of what you say and your signal.

ARROW 2: FIRMING

When students make mistakes, you correct them. A correction may occur during any part of the teacher presentation that calls for students to respond. Here are the rules for corrections:

- You correct a mistake as soon as you hear it.
- A mistake on oral responses is saying the wrong thing or not responding.

In step 4, students may not say anything or may not correctly answer the question, "What part names?" You correct as soon as you hear the mistake. You do not wait until students finish responding before correcting.

To correct, say the correct response and then repeat the task they missed.

> Teacher: A little dog is running down the street. What part names?
> Some students: *A little dog is . . .*
> Teacher: **A little dog.** That's the part that names. Listen: A little dog is running down the street. What part names?

Remember, wherever there's an oral task that involves all the students, there's a place where students may make mistakes.

Sometimes one step in the exercise involves a series of oral tasks.

4. New sentence: A little dog (pause) is running down the street. What part names? (Signal.) *A little dog.*
- New sentence: A boy and a girl (pause) are running down the street. What part names? (Signal.) *A boy and a girl.*
- New sentence: Two girls (pause) are eating ice cream. What part names? (Signal.) *Two girls.*
- New sentence: The man and the boy (pause) ate ice cream. What part names? (Signal.) *The man and the boy.* (Repeat step 4 until firm.)

After correcting any mistakes within this series of tasks, you would return to the beginning of step 4 and present the entire step.

The note **(Repeat step until firm)** occurs when students must correctly produce a series of responses. When you "repeat until firm," you follow these steps:

1) Correct the mistake. (Tell the answer and repeat the task that was missed.)
2) Return to the beginning of the specified step and present the entire step.

"Repeating until firm" provides information you need about the students. When the students made the mistake, you told the answer. Did they remember the answer? Would they now be able to perform the step correctly? The repeat-until-firm procedure provides you with answers to these questions. You present the context in which the mistake occurred, and the students can show you through their responses whether or not the correction worked, whether or not they are **firm.**

The repeat-until-firm direction appears only on the most critical parts of new teaching exercises. It usually focuses on knowledge that is very important for later work. In the activity above, for instance, you want to make sure that the students understand how to identify the part that names. However, if you're quite sure that the mistake was a "glitch" and does not mean that the students lack understanding, don't follow the repeat-until-firm direction.

The specified responses for some tasks are not what some students might say. Expect variability on some group responses. Accept any reasonable wording.

If you want to hold students to the wording that is in the script (which is not necessary for tasks that can be reasonably answered in other ways), say something like, "That's right." Then say the response you want. "Everybody, say it that way."

As a rule, if more than one answer is possible for the task you presented and you know that the students' answers are reasonable, don't bother with a correction. Just move on to the next part of the teacher script.

ARROW 3: PACING YOUR PRESENTATION

You should pace your verbal presentation at a normal speaking rate—as if you were telling somebody something important.

The most typical mistake teachers make is going too slowly or talking as if to preschoolers.

The arrows for number 3 on the diagram show two ways to pace your presentation for activities where students write or get involved in touching or finding parts of their workbook page. The first is a ✔ mark. That's a note to check what the students are doing. The second is a note to **(Observe students and give feedback).**

A ✔ requires only a second or two. If you are positioned close to several "average performing" students, check whether they are performing. If they are, proceed with the presentation.

The **(Observe students and give feedback)** direction implies a more elaborate response. You sample more students and you give feedback, not only to individual students, but to the group. Here are the basic rules for what to do and what not to do when you observe and give feedback.

1) Make sure that you are not at the front of the class when you present the directions for tasks that involve observing student performance. When you direct students to copy a sentence, move from the front of the room to a place where you can quickly sample the performance of low, middle and high performers.

2) As soon as students start to work, start observing. As you observe, make comments to the whole class. Focus these comments on students who are (a) following directions, (b) working quickly, (c) working accurately. "Wow, a couple of students are almost finished. I haven't seen one mistake so far."

3) When students raise their hand to indicate that they are finished, acknowledge them. (When you acknowledge that they are finished, they are to put their hand down.)

4) If you observe mistakes, do **not** provide a great deal of individual help. Point out any mistakes, but do not do the work for the students. Point to the problem and say, "I think you made a mistake. Look at the first word in your sentence." If students are not following instructions that you gave, tell them, "You're supposed to use capital letters only at the beginning of the sentences. You have to listen very carefully to the instructions."

5) Do not wait for the slowest students to complete the activities before presenting the work check (during which students correct their work and fix up any mistakes). A good rule early in the program is to allow a **reasonable amount of time** for students to complete their work. You can usually use the middle performers as a gauge for what is reasonable. As you observe that they are completing their work, announce, "Okay, you have about 10 seconds more to finish up." At the end of that time, continue in the exercise.

6) Circulate among the students and make sure that they fix up any mistakes you identify.

7) If you observe a serious problem that is not unique to only the lowest performers, tell the class, "Stop. We seem to have a serious problem." Repeat the part of the exercise that gives them information about what they are to do. (**Note:** Do not provide "new teaching." Simply repeat the part of the exercise that gives them the information they need and reassign the work. "Let's see who can get it this time . . . .")

Managing Writing Activities

The writing activity in each lesson (beginning with lesson 10) is presented after the work on specific skills. Most writing activity involves the following:

- an introduction
- writing
- oral reading of some passages
- checks for specific criteria

The last two steps of this process (reading passages and checking them) **account for possibly half of what students learn about writing.** Students learn from the good models that are read and from the mistakes in the models that are read. The oral reading of passages, therefore, is extremely important in shaping the students' understanding of how to apply what they have learned to specific writing assignments.

The checks that follow the oral reading are also very important because they provide students with practice in applying multiple criteria to their passages.

Effective management techniques for presenting writing assignments assure that students will learn from the models and will become facile at checking their own work. These techniques also reduce the amount of time you spend marking papers. Following writing assignments, you mark papers (which is a job that can become overwhelming because students write a lot).

Here are the basic rules to follow as students write:

1. Read passages as students are writing. If you become practiced at moving from student to student, you can read most of what students write as they are writing. A good technique is to make a line on the paper to mark what you've already read.

2. Refer to the criteria given in the instructions when commenting on what students have written. If students did not follow the directions, tell them which directions they didn't follow. "You were supposed to start each sentence by naming someone or something. I think some of your sentences have problems. Read over what you've written and see if you can fix it up."

3. Do not spend a lot of time with one student. There will be time for fix-ups later. Don't stand around as a student tries to find and correct the problem. Instead, observe other students and possibly return to the problem student later.

4. For passages that have problems, put a dot in the margin for each line that has a problem. When you read the passage later, you can scan the part you've already read to see if the mistake has been corrected.

5. Make frequent comments to the class. These comments should focus on what students are doing well and specific mistakes observed in several students' writing. "Wow, we have some good opening sentences that tell the main thing about the group" . . . "Watch how you punctuate the sentence that tells what Bob said."
   If students have had problems with a particular skill in the past and are doing well, make comments to the class. "You are doing a super job with sentences that begin with the part that tells when."

6. Do not wait for all students to complete their passage. Allow a reasonable amount of time (based on the performance of a slower but industrious student's performance) for students to complete the passage. Then tell students to stop writing. (It's a good idea to let them know a minute or two beforehand how much time they have left.) If you wait for all students to finish, students' writing rate will not improve greatly because there's no payoff for writing faster. If writing rate is a problem, reinforce students who improve and who complete assignments within a reasonable time period. Students who do not finish on time should finish the assignment at another time during the day. Although schedules often make it difficult to work with these students, you may be able to schedule a time during which other students are engaged in independent work, or it may be possible to assign higher-performing students to work with slower students during the make-up time.

7. Praise improvement. Make announcements to the class. Be sure to praise improvement of the low performers. They should understand that they are not failing to meet your expectations. "Well, you sure wrote a lot more today than you did last time. Good writing. Keep it up."

As Students Read Their Passages

Following the writing, you will call on a few students to read what they've written. They haven't checked their work yet, and the reading should be presented within this context. You will point out specific problems and engage the class in attending to mistakes as well as to aspects that are good.

Here are the general rules to follow:

1. Provide constant reminders to students about the context: "Remember, some of the passages may have problems, but we're reading them before they are checked over and fixed up. If we find mistakes, that's good, because the writer will know what has to be fixed up."

2. Call on a mix of higher- and lower-performing students. However, do not call on lower performers unless you know that what they've written has very few mistakes. (You've read the passage or most of it.)

3. Make sure that students attend to the passages that are read and identify specific problems. (You direct students to raise their hand if they hear a problem.) A good technique is to model the behavior that you want students to perform. When **you** hear a problem, raise your hand. You may provide some kind of reinforcement for students who identify problems correctly. "When I hear a problem, I'm going to raise my hand, but not right away. If at least ten hands are up before I raise my hand, I'll call on a student to tell about the problem. If the student is right, the whole class receives a bonus." (Set a goal for bonus points. After the class has earned so many bonus points, the students receive a special treat of some sort.)

4. Establish a general rule that students are not to make fun of another student's writing or become derogatory. "Remember, everybody makes mistakes. We're reading the stories so we can help each other fix up the mistakes. We won't make fun of you if you happen to make a mistake, and you will not make fun of somebody else who makes a mistake. At the end of the year, you'll all be able to look back at the mistakes you made at first and wonder how you could have made them."

5. Do not let mistakes go by without comment. Students will not learn to apply the skills and criteria if they are apparently unimportant. Teachers sometimes feel that they don't want to emphasize the negative, and they therefore don't comment on mistakes. This procedure is ineffective. You will not help students learn if you demonstrate that they do not have to apply what is learned. If none of the students identifies a problem, raise your hand and you identify the problem.

6. Make appropriate positive comments about passages that have been read. But make sure that you base your judgment on whether the assignment **follows the directions that you provided.** Also praise improvement. "I'm impressed with what Josh wrote. It's a lot longer than the last story he wrote and nearly all the sentences were good. Keep it up, Josh."

7. Tell students how to correct any mistake, including mistakes that are not specifically associated with the directions. If the student writes, "He didn't have no apples," tell the student how to correct the sentence.

   "Here's how you could fix up that sentence. He didn't have **any** apples."

   If students use awkward prepositions or phrases, tell them a better way. For example, if a student writes, "A man in a long beard stood next to the car," say something like, "Here's a better way to say that: A man **with** a long beard stood next to the car." Follow the general rule that you should tell students how to correct any awkward parts of sentences.

8. Do not make a great fuss about passages that incorporate newly taught skills unless the directions call for such incorporation. For example, as students are learning to construct sentences that begin with the part of the predicate that tells when, some students may use these sentences in their passage. The same is true of direct quotes and the other skills that are taught. The best response is something like this: "Tim's passage had sentences that begin with the part that tells when. In a few lessons, you'll all be doing that. But if your sentences begin with the subject, your sentences are just fine."

9. Do not praise any sentences or passages that are in violation of the directions for the exercise. If what the student wrote is in violation of the directions, tell the student, "You made up an ending to the story about Tom and Linda, but that's not what the directions told you to do. You'll have a chance to write endings later in the program, but you have to follow the directions."

   If you don't hold students to the directions, it won't be long before students totally ignore directions. If some students write involved sentences of a type that has not been introduced, warn the other students. "Amy told what Bill said, but you don't know how to punctuate those sentences yet, so you shouldn't be writing them."

AS STUDENTS CHECK THEIR PASSAGES

The final activity involves the checks that appear in the writing assignment. The checks are not always the same, and there are never more than three checks. However, the checks become very general near the end of the program. Here are the checks from a later lesson:

   Check 1. Did you tell what Ron did and said in the first picture?
   Check 2. Did you tell about four or more important things that happened in the missing picture?
   Check 3. Are all your sentences written correctly?

Students are directed to read their passage for each check.

Here are procedures for making the checks effective:

1. Establish a procedure for making the checks important. An effective plan is to tell the students that, after each check, you'll pick three papers to test for that check. For each paper that has been fixed up or that meets the criterion for the check, everybody in the class earns 1 point. Write the number of points the class earns on the chalkboard. Repeat the procedure for each check, looking at three different papers and again writing the number of points on the chalkboard.

   If some of the students are low performers, you may want to check their papers only on criteria you know they will meet. It's important, however, to make your checking practices appear to be random, so that students do not know when their papers will be checked.

   To make the system even more potent, you may include a provision that, if the class earns 9 points (3 points for each check), you'll award 5 bonus points.

   The points can be used for a weekly treat of some sort. The treat should have a price tag of 7 points per lesson. If students have three writing periods per week, the price tag is 21 points.

2. As students check their work, circulate among them and look at their papers. If you observe a sentence that has not been corrected, give the student general information about the problem. Do not identify the sentence with the problem. Say something like, "The first part of your paragraph—where you tell about the first picture—has a problem. Read it for Check 2. See if you can find it and fix it up."

3. Do not hover over the student as he or she tries to find and correct the problem. Observe other students. Then possibly return to see whether the student has found the problem sentence.

4. Students who have not completed their paragraph should make a line in the margin to show how much they have written. They check what they have written. Later, after they complete the passage, they hand it in without the last part being checked.

MARKING PAPERS

After students complete their checks, they hand in their papers. You mark them. If the checks and your observations are performed well, it's a lot easier to mark the papers. The line you marked indicates how much of each paper you've already checked. Any dots in the margin indicate sentences that had problems. By scanning first to see if problem sentences were corrected and then reading the remainder of the paper, you should be able to process each paper in less than a minute.

The comments you write on the paper should help students learn and reinforce good practices. Here are some procedures that work well:

1. Correct improper grammar by writing the correct words above the incorrect ones. *Note:* Use this procedure only with respect to grammatical constructions that are not taught in Level C. For instance: She walked slow. Adverb usage is not taught in Level C. Correct the word **slow** in pencil. She walked **slowly.**

2. Do not penalize students for **all** spelling mistakes. Words that appear in the vocabulary box for each assignment should be spelled correctly; however, a student's paper may have many "invented" spellings. A good rule is to hold the students accountable for any "spelling words" they should know and any words in the vocabulary box. You can write **S** or **Sp** above these words to indicate they are misspelled. If you wish to show the student the spelling of other

words that are misspelled, write the word in pencil above the misspelled word. By writing it in pencil, you make it easy for the student to erase the misspelled word, fix up the word and erase the word you wrote.

3. Use a general code for indicating other mistakes. You can refer to the checks and indicate in the margin the lines that have problems. Write (1), (2) or (3) to indicate which check was violated (Check 1, Check 2 or Check 3). Do **not** mark the part of the sentence that has a problem.

   At lesson 50, you can introduce another possible code that involves two symbols: **P** and **?.**

   P indicates that there is a punctuation problem—capitals, periods, commas, quote marks, run on sentences.

   ? indicates that something is unclear, an important detail is missing, or there's a clarity problem (usually associated with pronouns, tense or agreement problems). For tense and agreement problems, you may write something like **? verb** so the student has more specific information about where to search for the problem.

   The reason for not marking the specific words or parts that have problems is to make sure that students become facile at reading what they have written for multiple criteria. The two symbols **P** and **?** are actually a test for mechanics (**P**) and a test for communication clarity (**?**). Writing is largely an inference game that involves using mechanical devices and viewing the work from the standpoint of the reader to design an effective communication. A large part of the game is trying to figure out what the problems are with what you've written. The codes provide students with a manageable introduction to this game.

4. Make comments on the paper. You may use letter grades or just comments. Try to focus on improvement even if a paper has serious problems.
   Much better. Watch run-ons.

   or

   Good checking for 1. Be careful on Check 2.

   For good papers, write comments such as:
   Super! or Great job!

5. Try to return students' papers before the next scheduled language lesson. Students are to fix up any mistakes before you begin the next lesson. They are to show you that they have fixed up the mistakes. A good practice is to tell the students to put their corrected papers on their desk at the beginning of the next language lesson. You can either check the fix-ups then, or you can do it as part of your observation when students write their passage for the current lesson.

Here is a copy of a student's paper when the student handed in the paper. Note the three dots on the paper. These dots indicate errors. The student fixed up one error before handing in the paper. Also note the line which indicates the last line the teacher had read during the lesson.

Jill threw a ball to Robert. Robert jumped up. The ball goes over his head. It rolled down a hill toward a skunk. Rover chased the ball. the skunk made a biggest stink. Robert and Jill held their nose to keep out the terabul smell

Here is a copy of the paper after the teacher marks it. Note the **Sp** written over the misspelled word. This word appeared in the vocabulary box.

The word **terrible** is written over **terabul** since this word neither appears in the vocabulary box nor was in an earlier spelling lesson. The (1) in the margin refers to Check 1 which dealt with capitals and periods. The (1) indicates that there is an error regarding capitals or periods on that line. The (2) in the margin refers to check 2 which dealt with writing what happened, not what is happening.

Much Better
Keep working hard.

•		Jill threw a ball to Robert.
•②		Robert jumped up. The ball goes over his head. It rolled down a hill toward a skunk. Rover chased
•		the ball. The skunk made a biggest stink. Robert and Jill held their nose to keep out
①		the terrible smell

SHAPING BETTER WRITING

Sometimes students will write as little as possible. This tendency usually indicates that they are getting punished for writing more than the necessary minimum. (Students tend to write less if all spelling mistakes are marked and if they are held accountable for correctly punctuating sentence forms that have not been taught.)

Here are procedures for shaping better writing and a greater amount of writing:

1. Read selections to the class that are good examples of what you want students to do. Beginning in lesson 33, the program specifies that you will select and read what several students wrote for the preceding assignment. Do not read passages that are flowery, that contain sentence types that have not yet been introduced, or that violate any of the checks. As a rule, select passages that contain more that the minimum number of sentences. Point that out as you read the selection. "This next selection has six sentences. Listen . . ."

After reading a well-written selection, refer to any checks that gave **some of the students** problems. "Did you notice that Amy had three sentences that begin with the part that tells when? Listen again . . ."

Try to read at least one passage written by a lower performer. Make sure, however, that it meets the checks and does not contain sentences that have serious grammatical problems. "Here's a paper written by Mark. It's a little short, but it does a very good job of meeting all the checks. Listen . . ."

2. Post papers of the week. A good plan is to have a bulletin board with two labels: **Super** and **Good**. Students select their best paper for the week and you post it under the appropriate heading. Tell students whose papers are posted under **Good** that if they keep working hard, they'll have papers that are super. When a student who has never been posted under **Super** moves up to this category, acknowledge the student's performance. "This is the first time we have one of Kimberly's papers in the **Super** class. But I'll bet it won't be the last. Good work, Kimberly."

Encourage students. Read the posted papers.

SUMMARY

The procedures are designed to—

1. Provide students with practice in successfully using the process of writing—initial writing, checking, and rewriting according to specific checks.
2. Provide them with a mind-set that anticipates possible problems associated with the criteria that are used to judge their works.
3. Allow them to fix up papers before handing them in.
4. Provide them with motivation to write more and to write better.
5. Allow them to succeed.

The procedures will also make your work easier. You'll spend less time reading papers, correcting them, and trying to shape writing behavior.

Follow the procedures.

Tracks

This section describes the major tracks developed in Level C. Each track deals with a significant topic. Activities from the track appear on a large range of lessons. On a particular lesson, activities from more than one track are presented to students. See the scope-and-sequence chart on pages 2 and 3. The major tracks are:

Sentence Analysis
Mechanics
Editing
Reporting—Based on Pictures
Inferring—Based on Pictures
Clarity—Based on Pictures
Extended Writing

Sentence Analysis

Sentence-analysis activities are dispersed throughout Level C. Here's a summary of the sentence-analysis skills that students learn. Students learn to—

Identify the subject and predicate of declarative sentences
Identify one-word and two-word verbs
Identify pronouns
Identify nouns
Identify adjectives

The sequence of introduction, although different from that of traditional approaches, has been designed to show students how to distinguish one part of speech from another and how to use sentence analysis when writing.

SUBJECT-PREDICATE

Students first learn to identify the subject and predicate of regular-order sentences. Later, they learn about sentences that begin with the part of the predicate that tells **when.** The work on subject-predicate sets the stage for learning about parts of speech. For the sentences the students analyze, the verb is always the first word or words in the predicate. The subject either consists of a pronoun or contains a noun. Therefore, the subject–predicate analysis sets the stage for learning verbs, pronouns, and nouns. In lesson 1, students are introduced to subject–predicate. For the first exercises, they work only with the subject, which is referred to as **the part that names.** Here's the exercise from lesson 1.

Part B	Circle the part of each sentence that names.
	1. The old man went to the store.
	2. The man and the boy went to the store.
	3. The horse jumped over the fence.

1. Everybody, pencils down.
   You're going to learn about sentences.
2. Here's a sentence: **The woman** (pause) went to the store. Say that sentence. (Signal.) *The woman went to the store.* (Repeat step 2 until firm.)
3. Listen: **The woman** (pause) went to the store.
   Here's the part of the sentence that names: the woman.
   Listen: The woman went to the store. Everybody, what part names? (Signal.) *The woman.*
4. New sentence: **The old man** (pause) went to the store. What part names? (Signal.) *The old man.*
   • New sentence: The man and the boy (pause) went to the store. What part names? (Signal.) *The man and the boy.*
   • New sentence: A man (pause) ran in the park. What part names? (Signal.) *A man.*

• New sentence: Two girls (pause) ran in the park. What part names? (Signal.) *Two girls.*
   (Repeat step 4 until firm.)
5. New sentence: A big dog is running in the park. What part names? (Signal.) *A big dog.*
   • New sentence: The rabbit and the squirrel are running in the park. What part names? (Signal.) *The rabbit and the squirrel.*
   • New sentence: Four yellow birds flew to a tree. What part names? (Signal.) *Four yellow birds.*
   • New sentence: A bird and an elephant ate dinner. What part names? (Signal.) *A bird and an elephant.*
   • New sentence: A gray elephant went swimming in the lake. What part names? (Signal.) *A gray elephant.*
   (Repeat step 5 until firm.)
6. Everybody, find part B. ✔
   Touch each sentence as I read it.
   Sentence 1: The old man went to the store.
   Sentence 2: The man and the boy went to the store.
   Sentence 3: The horse jumped over the fence.
   Make a circle around the part of each sentence that names. Circle the part that names. Raise your hand when you're finished.
   (Observe students and give feedback.)
7. Let's check your work. Make an **X** next to any item you missed.
   • Sentence 1: The old man went to the store. Everybody, say the part you circled. (Signal.) *The old man.*
   • Sentence 2: The man and the boy went to the store. Say the part you circled. (Signal.) *The man and the boy.*
   • Sentence 3: The horse jumped over the fence. Say the part you circled. (Signal.) *The horse.*
8. Raise your hand if you got no items wrong. Super job.

- Everyone else, fix up any mistakes you made in part B.
  (Observe students and give feedback.)

Teaching Notes

- In step 1 of the exercise, you direct students to put their pencils down. This step occurs in many exercises. When you present these exercises, make sure that the students follow your directions. These directions are important because you do not want students to write in steps 1 through 5. During the presentation of these steps, students listen and respond orally.

  Position yourself among the students and move around as you present the exercise so that you can observe whether students are following directions.

- Your voice inflection is very important in the first part of this exercise. For the first two sentences, stress the part that names and pause:

The old man (pause) went to the store.

  For the next three sentences, pause, but don't stress the first part.

  For the last five sentences, don't pause or stress. Simply say the sentences in a conversational tone.

- Make sure that the students are very firm on step 5 before presenting the workbook activity. If students make any mistakes in part 5, follow the firming procedure.

Tell them the answer as soon as you hear a mistake.

Repeat the task they missed. (Say the sentence and ask, "What part names?")

Go back to the beginning of step 5 and run the step so that all students respond correctly.

If students are firmed the first time this type of exercise is presented, they will have a much easier time with later exercises.

- In steps 7 and 8, you direct students to check their work and to fix up any mistakes.

They are to make an X next to any item they missed. They are to fix up mistakes in any sentences marked with an X (step 8). This procedure is followed throughout the program. The students are **not** to fix up the mistakes as you conduct the work check. They are simply to mark incorrect items with an X. After the exercise, allow students reasonable time to fix up the mistakes. For the exercise above, a reasonable amount of time should be no more than half a minute. It you allow too much time, students will not try to work fast and will not tend to remember the correct answers for the items they missed. If done correctly, the work check will shape the students' memories for missed items.

In lesson 4, after students have identified the part that names for three lessons, students learn that the rest of the sentence **tells more** about what is named in the subject. Here's the exercise from lesson 6. Students orally respond to some sentences, then circle the part that names and underline the part that tells more.

Part C Circle the part that names. Underline the part that tells more.

1. Three tall girls sat on a horse.

2. They rode the horse across the field.

3. Their horse jumped over a fence.

4. A girl and her horse went across a stream.

5. She rested under a tree.

---

1. Everybody, pencils down. Find part C. For each sentence in part C, you're going to **circle** the part that names and **underline** the part that tells more.
2. Everybody, touch sentence 1.
   Three tall girls sat on a horse. Say the part of the sentence that names. (Signal.) *Three tall girls.*
   • Say the part of the sentence that tells more. (Signal.) *Sat on a horse.* (Repeat step 2 until firm.)
3. You're going to circle the part that names. Listen to the sentence again: Three tall girls sat on a horse. Circle the part that names. ✔
   • Everybody, read the words you circled. (Signal.) *Three tall girls.*
   • Now underline the part of sentence 1 that tells more. (Observe students and give feedback.)
   • Everybody, read the words you underlined. (Signal.) *Sat on a horse.*
4. Touch sentence 2.
   They rode the horse across the field. Say the part of the sentence that names. (Signal.) *They.*
   • Say the part of the sentence that tells more. (Signal.) *Rode the horse across the field.* (Repeat step 4 until firm.)

5. Circle the part of the sentence that names and underline the part that tells more. (Observe students and give feedback.)
   • Everybody, read the part of sentence 2 that names. (Signal.) *They.*
   • Read the part that tells more. (Signal.) *Rode the horse across the field.*
6. I'll read the rest of the sentences in part C. Touch each sentence as I read it.
   Sentence 3: Their horse jumped over a fence.
   Sentence 4: A girl and her horse went across a stream.
   Sentence 5: She rested under a tree.
   • For each sentence, circle the part of the sentence that names. Underline the part that tells more. Do it now. Raise your hand when you're finished. (Observe students and give feedback.)
7. Let's check your work. Make an **X** next to any item you missed.
   • Sentence 3. What part names? (Signal.) *Their horse.*
   What part tells more? (Signal.) *Jumped over a fence.*
   • Sentence 4. What part names? (Signal.) *A girl and her horse.*
   What part tells more? (Signal.) *Went across a stream.*
   • Sentence 5. What part names? (Signal.) *She.*
   What part tells more? (Signal.) *Rested under a tree.*
8. Raise your hand if you got no items wrong. Great job.
   • Raise your hand if you got 1 item wrong. Good work.
   • Fix up any mistakes you made in part C. (Observe students and give feedback.)

Beginning in lesson 11, students apply the procedure of circling the part that names and underlining the part that tells more to sentences in a passage. All the sentences begin with the part that names.

Beginning in lesson 17, students analyze passages to identify the sentences. The sentences have no capitals or periods. Students identify the part that names and the part that tells more to figure out where each sentence starts and ends. They then capitalize the first word and put a period at the end of each sentence. Here's the exercise from lesson 17.

Part B   Put in capitals and periods. Circle the part of each sentence that names.

A red kite floated into the sky the wind blew the kite three brown ducks flew near the kite the kite went behind some clouds it went so high that nobody could see it.

   Somebody forgot to put capitals and periods in the sentences.

2. Look at the first words in the paragraph and figure out what the first sentence names.
- Everybody, what does it name? (Signal.) *A red kite.*
  Circle **a red kite.** ✔
- The first sentence tells more about a red kite. (Call on a student:) Say the rest of the sentence that starts with **a red kite.** *Floated into the sky.*
- Everybody, put a period after the word **sky.** Start the next sentence with a capital **T.** ✔

3. Look at the first words in the second sentence and figure out what that sentence names.
- Everybody, what does it name? (Signal.) *The wind.*
  Circle **the wind.** ✔
- Everybody, say the words that tell more about the wind. (Signal.) *Blew the kite.*
- Put a period after the word **kite.** Start the next sentence with a capital **T.** ✔

4. Fix up the rest of this paragraph. Make sure each sentence begins with a capital and ends with a period. Circle the part of each sentence that names. Raise your hand when you're finished. (Observe students and give feedback.)

5. Let's check your work. Make an **X** over anything you missed.
- First sentence: You should have circled **a red kite.** A red kite floated into the sky, period.
- Next sentence: You should have circled **the wind.** Capital **T,** The wind blew the kite, period.
- Next sentence: You should have circled **three brown ducks.** Capital **T,** Three brown ducks flew near the kite, period.
- Next sentence: You should have circled **the kite.** Capital **T,** The kite went behind some clouds, period.
- Next sentence: You should have circled **it.** Capital **I,** It went so high that nobody could see it, period.

6. Raise your hand if you made no mistakes. Great job.
- Everybody else, fix up any mistakes you made in part B.
  (Observe students and give feedback.)

Teaching Notes

This type of exercise is very difficult for students who have not learned to analyze sentences with respect to subject and predicate. Students who understand subject-predicate may still have some problems, but you can correct mistakes by referring to what they know. They learn that placement of capitals and periods is not a random activity.

In later lessons, students fix up passages in which **some** of the sentences do not have capitals or periods. This editing context is similar to the situation in which students write and edit their own work.

In lesson 22, students are taught that the part of the sentence that names is the **subject.** Here's the first part of that exercise.

1. Pencils down. You're going to learn about the **subject** of a sentence. Listen: The **subject** of a sentence is the part of the sentence that names. Everybody, what do we call the part of the sentence that names? (Signal.) *The subject.*
2. Listen: Six little dogs barked loudly. Everybody, what's the part that names? (Signal.) *Six little dogs.*
• So what's the subject of that sentence? (Signal.) *Six little dogs.*
• Listen: A boy and a girl walked in the park. What's the subject of that sentence? (Signal.) *A boy and a girl.*
• Listen: They went home. What's the subject of that sentence? (Signal.) *They.*
(Repeat step 2 until firm.)

3. Listen: That shirt is beautiful. What's the subject of that sentence? (Signal.) *That shirt.*
• Listen: My mother and her friend talked on the phone. What's the subject of that sentence? (Signal.) *My mother and her friend.*
• Listen: Her face and her hands got dirty. What's the subject of that sentence? (Signal.) *Her face and her hands.*
(Repeat step 3 until firm.)

Teaching Notes

Sentences are grouped so that you can firm responses (steps 2 and 3). Within each group are greatly different sentences. One has a subject containing more than one word (six little dogs); one has a subject that names more than one entity (a boy and a girl); one has a pronoun for a subject (they). This variation assures that students do not learn serious misrules about the nature of the subject and assume that a subject must have a certain arrangement or number of words.

Learning the new word **subject** for the part that names is not difficult for students. They already know the concept (the part that names). Learning the new label involves no new understanding. It is simply identifying something that is familiar with a new word.

Make sure that you firm students in step 2 and step 3 before presenting the written work that follows the oral activity.

In lesson 24, students learn to identify the part that tells more as the **predicate.** In later lessons, students continue to use the subject-predicate skills. Some exercises present sentence parts, and students identify the parts as either subject or predicate. For some exercises, students are presented with subjects in one column and predicates in the second column. They combine the parts to create unique sentences.

Subject-predicate is reviewed in editing exercises during the 25 through 57 lesson range. In lesson 58, students are introduced to the part of the predicate that tells when. They make a line over the words in the predicate that tell when. At first, all sentences begin with the subject:

The boy cleaned the garage after breakfast.

All the people clapped when the movie ended.

In lesson 62, after working on the words that tell when for five lessons, students are shown that sentences may begin with part of the predicate. For this exercise, the worksheet items show the same sentence written first in the regular order and then beginning with part of the predicate. For each sentence, students circle the subject, underline the predicate, and make a line over the words that tell when.

In the lessons that follow lesson 62, students learn the rule that, if the sentence begins with part of the predicate, a comma is needed just before the subject. While this rule is sometimes violated in modern style, the violations are "exceptions" that are taught to the students in later levels of *Reasoning and Writing.* In Level C, the rule is treated without exception, even for parts that are relatively short, such as: Yesterday, we went shopping. The reason for the "no exception" procedure is to show students the relationship between sentence parts and punctuation. The regular-order sentence that begins with the subject is the "model." It is written without a comma. All the parts of the regular-order sentence are present. In the predicate-first sentence, a part has been moved, so a comma is needed. An understanding of these points is important for many aspects of grammatical analysis that occur in later levels.

In lesson 65, students rewrite sentences that begin with the part of the predicate that tells when.

Part C

- Our dog barked when the man walked by.
- When the man walked by, our dog barked.

Rules: Start with a capital letter.
Write the part that tells when.
Make a comma and write the rest of the sentence.
End the sentence with a period.

1. They went swimming in the morning.
2. We talked softly while the baby slept.
3. The cook took a nap after lunch.

- You're going to rewrite sentences so they begin with the part of the predicate that tells when. Remember the rule: If a sentence begins with part of the predicate, you should have a comma just before the subject.
2. Touch the first sentence in the rule box. Our dog barked when the man walked by. The subject is circled. The predicate is underlined. And there is a line over the part of the predicate that tells when.
- Everybody, read the part of the predicate that tells when. (Signal.) *When the man walked by.*
- Below is the sentence rewritten so it begins with the part that tells when. When the man walked by, our dog barked. The rules for rewriting the sentences are in the box. Here they are: Start with a capital letter. Write the part that tells when. Make a comma and write the rest of the sentence. End the sentence with a period. That's how you're going to do it.

3. Touch item 1. They went swimming in the morning.
   - Everybody, what's the subject? (Signal.) *They.*
   - What's the whole predicate? (Signal.) *Went swimming in the morning.*
   - What's the part that tells when? (Signal.) *In the morning.*
   - Rewrite that sentence so it begins with the part of the predicate that tells when. Start with a capital. Write the part that tells when. Then make a comma. Then write the rest of the sentence. Put a period at the end. Raise your hand when you're finished with sentence 1. (Observe students and give feedback.)
   - Everybody, read the sentence you wrote. (Signal.) *In the morning, they went swimming.*
   - Check your work. Here's what you should have written: In the morning, comma, small **t,** they went swimming, period. Raise your hand if you got it right.
4. Item 2: We talked softly while the baby slept. Everybody, what's the subject? (Signal.) *We.*
   - What's the predicate? (Signal.) *Talked softly while the baby slept.*
   - What's the part that tells when? (Signal.) *While the baby slept.*
   - Your turn: Rewrite sentence 2 so it begins with the part of the predicate that tells when. Remember the comma just before the subject. Raise your hand when you're finished with sentence 2. (Observe students and give feedback.)
   - Everybody, read the sentence you wrote. (Signal.) *While the baby slept, we talked softly.*
   - Check your work. Here's what you should have written: While the baby slept, comma, small **w,** we talked softly, period.

5. Item 3: The cook took a nap after lunch.
   - Everybody, what's the subject? (Signal.) *The cook.*
   - What's the predicate? (Signal.) *Took a nap after lunch.*
   - What's the part that tells when? (Signal.) *After lunch.*
   - Your turn: Rewrite sentence 3 so it begins with the part of the predicate that tells when. Remember the comma just before the subject. Raise your hand when you're finished. (Observe students and give feedback.)
   - Everybody, read the sentence you wrote. (Signal.) *After lunch, the cook took a nap.*
   - Check your work. Here's what you should have written: After lunch, comma, small **t,** the cook took a nap, period.
6. Raise your hand if you wrote all the sentences correctly.
   - Everybody else, fix up any mistakes you made.

Teaching Notes

When you check each sentence (the last part of steps 3–5), you will refer to a "small" letter following the comma. The reason for this convention is that students sometimes capitalize the letter that follows the comma. (That is the same letter that is capitalized when the sentence is in the regular order.)

When you observe students writing the sentences, make sure they begin each sentence with a capital, include no other capitals, and end with a period.

After students learn how to write and punctuate sentences that begin with part of the predicate, they apply this skill to writing passages, starting with lesson 74. Here's the introduction to the first assignment that requires students to include these sentences in passages.

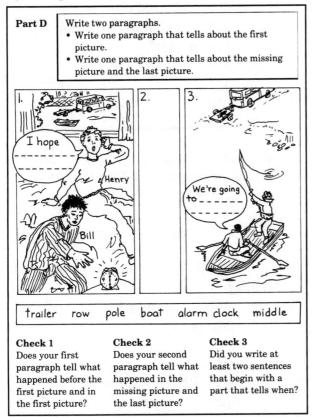

Part D Write two paragraphs.
- Write one paragraph that tells about the first picture.
- Write one paragraph that tells about the missing picture and the last picture.

trailer   row   pole   boat   alarm clock   middle

Check 1
Does your first paragraph tell what happened before the first picture and in the first picture?

Check 2
Does your second paragraph tell what happened in the missing picture and the last picture?

Check 3
Did you write at least two sentences that begin with a part that tells when?

- You've already written a paragraph that tells about these pictures. But this time you're going to write two paragraphs about these pictures and you'll write some sentences that begin with a part that tells when.
2. Look at the first picture.
   Raise your hand when you can say a sentence about the first picture that begins with a part that tells when.
- (Call on several students. Praise sentences such as: *When the alarm rang, Bill and Henry woke up; At six o'clock, the alarm clock rang; As the alarm clock rang, they got out of bed.*)

- Here are some sentences that begin with a part that tells when: When the alarm rang, Bill and Henry woke up; At six o'clock, the alarm clock rang; As the alarm clock rang, they got out of bed. All of those sentences begin with a part that tells when and tell what happened in the first picture.
3. Henry said something in the first picture. Raise your hand when you can finish the sentence he said.
- (Call on several students. Praise sentences such as: *I hope we catch some fish today or I hope the weather is good.*)
4. When you write your first paragraph, tell what happened **before** the first picture. Then tell what happened **in** the first picture. Start out by telling where they were and what they were doing before the alarm clock rang. You can also tell what they planned to do. Then write a sentence that tells what Henry said. Write at least one sentence that begins with a part that tells when. Remember how to punctuate that sentence. Raise your hand when you've written your paragraph about the first picture. You have 5 minutes.
(Observe students and give feedback.)

Teaching Notes

Check 3 focuses on sentences that begin with the part that tells when.

The subject-predicate analysis is important because it relates to sentences that students write, to punctuation, and to grammar. The notion of "converting" sentences to a basic form (subject first) is a major principle and a procedure for understanding grammar.

PARTS OF SPEECH

The parts of speech that are introduced in Level C are: verbs, pronouns, nouns, and adjectives. The work on both verbs and pronouns begins early in the program (lesson 4); however, students are not taught the labels until much later in the program (lesson 41).

VERB USAGE

The analysis of verbs moves in two directions. The first direction involves what the students write. Typically, students overuse sentences with progressive verbs.

They were going to the store.

Often, students have tense shifts.

**The man came into the room.
He sits down.**

The initial verb activities focus on these tendencies. The pictures that students refer to when writing show what **happened.** To tell about these pictures, students are to indicate what the characters **did,** not what they are doing or were doing.

This work begins in lesson 4. Students are presented with regular present-tense verbs. (The verbs are regular because they can be converted to past-tense verbs by adding **ed.**) Students write the past-tense verbs. Here's the exercise from lesson 4.

Part A	In each blank, write the word that tells what people did.	
	What people do	**What people did**
	1. burn	
	2. fill	
	3. push	
	4. lick	
	5. start	
	6. scratch	

2. The words in part A tell what people do. You can make the words tell what people **did** by adding the letters **e-d** to the end of each word. What letters do you add to make the words tell what people did? (Signal.) *E-d.*
3. Touch word 1. ✔
   What word? (Signal.) *Burn.*
   If you add the letters **e-d** to **burn,** the word says **burned.**
4. Touch word 2. What word? (Signal.) *Fill.*
   • What letters do you add to make the word tell what people did? (Signal.) *E-d.*
   • When you add **e-d,** you get a word that tells what people did. That word is **filled.** Spell **filled.** (Signal.) *F-i-l-l-e-d.*
5. Touch word 3.
   What word? (Signal.) *Push.*
   • **Push** tells what people **do.** Say the word that tells what they **did.** (Signal.) *Pushed.*
   • Spell **pushed.** (Signal.) *P-u-s-h-e-d.*
6. Go back to word 1.
   The word that tells what people do is **burn.** What's the word that tells what they did? (Signal.) *Burned.*
   • Write the word **burned** in the blank after **burn.**
   (Observe students and give feedback.)
7. Touch word 2.
   The word that tells what people do is **fill.** What's the word that tells what they did? (Signal.) *Filled.*
   • Write the word **filled** in the blank after **fill.**
   (Observe students and give feedback.)
8. Write the rest of the words that tell what people did. Raise your hand when you're finished.
   (Observe students and give feedback.)
9. Let's check your work. Make an **X** next to any item you missed.
   • Everybody, touch item 1.
   Say the word that tells what people did. (Signal.) *Burned.*
   Spell **burned.** (Signal.) *B-u-r-n-e-d.*

- Touch item 2.
  Say the word that tells what people did. (Signal.) *Filled.*
  Spell **filled.** (Signal.)   *F-i-l-l-e-d.*
- Touch item 3.
  Say the word that tells what people did. (Signal.) *Pushed.*
  Spell **pushed.** (Signal.)   *P-u-s-h-e-d.*
- Touch item 4.
  Say the word that tells what people did. (Signal.) *Licked.*
  Spell **licked.** (Signal.)   *L-i-c-k-e-d.*
- Touch item 5.
  Say the word that tells what people did. (Signal.) *Started.*
  Spell **started.** (Signal.)   *S-t-a-r-t-e-d.*
- Touch item 6.
  Say the word that tells what people did. (Signal.) *Scratched.*
  Spell **scratched.** (Signal.)
  S-c-r-a-t-c-h-e-d.

10. Raise your hand if you got no items wrong. Great job.
    - Raise your hand if you got 1 item wrong. Good work.
    - Fix up any mistakes you made in part A. (Observe students and give feedback.)

Teaching Notes

Students may be weak at spelling the words in step 9. If the responses are weak to the first two items, model the response you expect. Spell the words at a relatively slow rate (about 1/2 second per letter.) If you spell the words very fast, students will not be able to learn from your model.

Go back to item 1. My turn: Spell burned. B-U-R-N-E-D. Your turn: Spell burned.

Touch item 2. My turn to spell filled: F-I-L-L-E-D. Your turn: Spell filled.

In lesson 5, students review regular verbs and are introduced to a set of five irregular verbs. Students work with these five irregulars for four lessons. Then another set of irregulars is introduced. The procedure is repeated for three more sets of verbs. The verbs introduced include more common irregulars that students use when they write. Note, however, that the set of verbs is not exhaustive. Here's the student material from lesson 5.

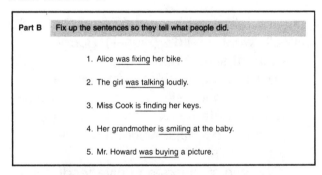

Part B	In each blank, write the word that tells what people did.				
1. find	found	6. buy	_____	11. dig	_____
2. give	gave	7. find	_____	12. buy	_____
3. buy	bought	8. dig	_____	13. have	_____
4. dig	dug	9. have	_____	14. give	_____
5. have	had	10. give	_____	15. find	_____

In lesson 6, students are presented with sentences that have progressive verbs (*was talking* or *is eating*). Students cross out both words of the verb and write the simple past-tense verb above the crossed-out words. Here's the first part of the exercise from lesson 6.

Part B	Fix up the sentences so they tell what people did.
	1. Alice <u>was fixing</u> her bike.
	2. The girl <u>was talking</u> loudly.
	3. Miss Cook <u>is finding</u> her keys.
	4. Her grandmother <u>is smiling</u> at the baby.
	5. Mr. Howard <u>was buying</u> a picture.

For things you'll write in this program, you'll tell what people **did,** not what they **were doing** or **are doing.** The words that are underlined in each sentence tell what people were doing or are doing. You're going to fix up those parts to tell what people did.

2. Sentence 1: Alice was fixing her bike. What words are underlined? (Signal.) *Was fixing.*
- That tells what she was doing. Here's the word that tells what she did: **fixed.** What word tells what she **did?** (Signal.) *Fixed.*
- Sentence 2: The girl was talking loudly. What words are underlined? (Signal.) *Was talking.*
- That tells what she was doing. Everybody, what word tells what she **did?** (Signal.) *Talked.*
- Sentence 3: Miss Cook is finding her keys. What words are underlined? (Signal.) *Is finding.*
- That tells what she is doing. What word tells what she **did?** (Signal.) *Found.*
- Sentence 4: Her grandmother is smiling at the baby. What words are underlined? (Signal.) *Is smiling.*
- That tells what she is doing. What word tells what she **did?** (Signal.) *Smiled.*
- Sentence 5: Mr. Howard was buying a picture. What words are underlined? (Signal.) *Was buying.*
- That tells what he was doing. What word tells what he **did?** (Signal.) *Bought.* (Repeat step 2 until firm.)
3. Your turn: Cross out the underlined words in each sentence. Above those words, write the word that tells what people did. Raise your hand when you're finished. (Observe students and give feedback.)

Teaching Notes

Make sure the students are firm on step 2 before they cross out the underlined words and write the simple past-tense verb. If students make mistakes in step 2, immediately tell them the correct answer. Repeat the task that they missed. If they make more than two mistakes in the series, repeat step 2 from the beginning.

Students apply the rule about past-tense verbs to their writing, starting in lesson 9. All sentences they write tell what illustrated characters **did.**

Starting in lesson 15, students discriminate between sentences that tell what people did and sentences that don't tell what they did. Some sentences tell what people were doing; some tell what people did. Students cross out the verbs that don't tell what people did and write the correct verb above it.

ran
He was running.

In lesson 18, students edit a passage for inappropriate verbs. Here's the passage and part of the exercise from lesson 18.

Part B   Make each sentence tell what a person or thing did.

Mark looked for a hidden treasure. He is going into his backyard with a shovel. He was digging for a long time. His shovel hit something hard. Mark was reaching into the hole. He pulled something out. He was finding a bone.

Does each sentence tell what a person or thing did?   X X X X

I'll read the instructions: Make each sentence tell what a person or thing did.
2. Touch the first sentence. Mark looked for a hidden treasure. That sentence tells what Mark did.
- I'll read the next sentence: He is going into his backyard with a shovel. Everybody, does that sentence tell what he did? (Signal.) *No.*
- Say the sentence so it tells what he did. (Signal.) *He went into his backyard with a shovel.*
- Cross out **is going** and write **went** above the crossed-out words. ✔
3. Everybody, touch the check box below the paragraph.
- I'll read the check: Does each sentence tell what a person or thing did? The **X**s in the box show how many mistakes there are in the paragraph. Count the **X**s and you'll know how many mistakes you should find. (Pause.)
- Everybody, how many mistakes? (Signal.) *Four.*

- Read the rest of the paragraph. Fix up any sentence that does not tell what Mark or his shovel did. Raise your hand when you're finished.

   (Observe students and give feedback.)

Teaching Notes

The student material has a check followed by four Xs. **Does each sentence tell what a person or thing did? (X X X X.)** The Xs provide you with a method for directing students to read the paragraph carefully. If a student missed one of the sentences, you might say something like, "You found three of the sentences that don't tell what a person or thing did, but there are four Xs. Look for the fourth sentence that is wrong and fix it up."

In the lessons following lesson 18, students work on variations of the editing exercise above. In lesson 20, the Xs are dropped, and students may tend to make the mistake of not finding all the sentences that have the wrong verb. If students get stuck, you may want to tell them how many sentences they overlooked. (Do not point out the improper sentences. You want to make students facile at rereading and correcting what is written.)

In lesson 31, students correct sentences that have verbs such as **bringed, gots, thinked.** The correct verbs for these items are words that students have studied as irregular verbs.

VERBS AS PARTS OF SPEECH

Starting with lesson 41, students are introduced to the label **verb** and analyze sentences to identify the verbs. Verbs are the first part of speech that students identify. The reason Level C introduces verbs first is that they are relatively easy for students to identify if they understand subject and predicate. In all the sentences they will work with, the verb is the first part of the predicate. Note that by using the subject-predicate analysis, students have less difficulty identifying verbs like **had** and **were** even though they don't specify an action.

Here's the introduction from lesson 41. All the sentences have one-word verbs.

EXERCISE 3 PARTS OF SPEECH
VERBS

1. Everybody, pencils down. Remember, every sentence has a verb. The verb is usually in the first part of the predicate.
- I'm going to say some sentences.
2. Listen: A dog ate lots of food. Say it. (Signal.) *A dog ate lots of food.*
- What's the subject? (Signal.) *A dog.*
- What's the predicate? (Signal.) *Ate lots of food.*
   What's the first word in the predicate? (Signal.) *Ate.*
- That's the verb.
- Listen: The girl threw a ball. Say it. (Signal.) *The girl threw a ball.*
- What's the subject? (Signal.) *The girl.*
- What's the predicate? (Signal.) *Threw a ball.*
   What's the first word in the predicate? (Signal.) *Threw.*
- That's the verb.
   (Repeat step 2 until firm.)

3. Listen: Boys and girls were in school. Say it. (Signal.) *Boys and girls were in school.*
   - What's the subject? (Signal.) *Boys and girls.*
   - What's the predicate? (Signal.) *Were in school.*
   - What's the verb? (Signal.) *Were.*
   - Listen: A bird flew. Say it. (Signal.) *A bird flew.*
   - What's the subject? (Signal.) *A bird.*
   - What's the predicate? (Signal.) *Flew.*
   - What's the verb? (Signal.) *Flew.*
   - Yes, **flew.** There's only one word in the predicate, so that word has to be the verb.
   (Repeat step 3 until firm.)

Part C

1. Six bottles were on the table.   3. Jane and Sue sat under a tree.
2. An old lion chased the rabbit.   4. His brother had a candy bar.

EXERCISE 4 VERBS

1. Everybody, find part C.
2. I'll read sentence 1: Six bottles were on the table.
   - What's the subject? (Signal.) *Six bottles.*
   - What's the predicate? (Signal.) *Were on the table.*
   - What's the verb? (Signal.) *Were.*
   - Sentence 2: An old lion chased the rabbit. What's the subject? (Signal.) *An old lion.*
   - What's the predicate? (Signal.) *Chased the rabbit.*
   - What's the verb? (Signal.) *Chased.*
3. Here are the instructions for part C: Circle the subject of each sentence. Underline the predicate. Then make a **V** above the verb. Remember, the verb is the first word of the predicate. Do the sentences now. Raise your hand when you're finished.
   (Observe students and give feedback.)

Teaching Notes

Make sure that students are firm on the verbal items in exercise 3 (steps 2 and 3) before you present the written activity in exercise 4.

Two-word verbs are introduced in lesson 44. Students are presented with one-word action verbs in isolation. For each verb, they identify the two-word verb. (For the verb **walked,** students say, *"was walking."*)

In lesson 45, students work from sentence pairs, such as

The boy walked to the store.

The boy was walking to the store.

For the first sentence, students circle the subject, underline the predicate, and write V above the verb. Then, they do the same thing for the second sentence (writing a V above **each** word of the verb.)

Following this introduction, students read sentences presented in the textbook and write the verb for each sentence. Some sentences have one-word verbs. Some have two-word verbs.

The last activities involving verbs in Level C require students to identify action verbs when they are presented in isolation. The workbook exercise presents a list of words, some of which are action verbs. Students circle the verbs.

Students continue to identify verbs throughout Level C as part of the teaching that introduces verbs, pronouns, nouns, and adjectives. After pronouns have been introduced, students circle the subject, underline the predicate, write V above each word of the verb and write P above each pronoun.

PRONOUN USAGE

Just as the verb activities move in two directions (writing and grammatical analysis) the activities that teach pronouns and their usage also go in two directions (writing usage and grammar). The major problem that students experience when using pronouns is that they create sentences that are not clear. The early pronoun activities in Level C address this problem with rules and with practice.

The first pronoun activity is introduced in lesson 7. The introduction demonstrates that specific pronouns can be used to replace names or nouns. Here's the introduction.

Part C	Fill in the blanks with **He** or **She**. Remember to start each sentence with a capital.

1.	The girl was running.	1.	_____ was running.
2.	My grandfather read a book.	2.	_____ read a book.
3.	Mary painted the wall.	3.	_____ painted the wall.
4.	Bill walked home.	4.	_____ walked home.
5.	My brother woke up.	5.	_____ woke up.
6.	His mother washed her hands.	6.	_____ washed her hands.

The person named in each sentence is underlined. You're going to change the underlined part to **he** or **she.**

2. Touch sentence 1.
   The girl was running. Say the part of the sentence that names. (Signal.) *The girl.*
   • Are you going to change **the girl** to **he** or **she?** (Signal.) *She.*
   • Say the sentence with **she.** (Signal.) *She was running.*
3. Touch sentence 2.
   My grandfather read a book. Say the part of the sentence that names. (Signal.) *My grandfather.*
   • Are you going to change **my grandfather** to **he** or **she?** (Signal.) *He.*
   • Say the sentence with **he.** (Signal.) *He read a book.*

4. Touch sentence 1 again.
   Sentence 1 says: The girl was running. We change **the girl** to **she.** Write **she** in the blank. Start with capital **S.** (Observe students and give feedback.)
5. Start the rest of the sentences in part C with **he** or **she.** Remember to start each sentence with a capital. Raise your hand when you're finished. (Observe students and give feedback.)

Teaching Notes

The initial exercise introduces the idea that the pronoun replaces the entire subject of a sentence—the noun and any words that precede it. Although students have a functional understanding of this substitution game, the set of examples they work with initially makes the nature of pronouns much more understandable than it is when students are taught a rule such as: Pronouns are used in place of nouns.

In lesson 9, students work on an activity similar to the one above except that some of the sentences have subjects that are replaced with **it: This book** was very funny. **It** was very funny.

Starting in lesson 14, students write the appropriate subject for the second sentence in a pair of related sentences.

Part A	Fill in the blanks with **He, She or It.**

1. Robert spent all morning cleaning his room. _____ put his dirty clothes in the laundry basket.
2. My sister went to the park. _____ played basketball with her friends for two hours.
3. The boat held four people. _____ had three sails.

   • Each item tells what the same person or thing did. We don't want to start all the sentences with the same name. So we start the second sentence in each item with **he, she** or **it.**
   2. Everybody, touch number 1. I'll read the first sentence: Robert spent all

morning cleaning his room. Everybody, what part of that sentence names? (Signal.) *Robert.*

- The next sentence also tells about Robert. What other word can we use to refer to **Robert?** (Signal.) *He.*
- So here's the next sentence: He put his dirty clothes in the laundry basket.

3. Touch number 2.
   I'll read the first sentence: My sister went to the park. Everybody, what part of that sentence names? (Signal.) *My sister.*

- The next sentence also tells about my sister. What other word can we use to refer to **my sister?** (Signal.) *She.*
- So here's the next sentence: She played basketball with her friends for two hours.

4. Touch number 3.
   I'll read the first sentence: The boat held four people. Everybody, what part of that sentence names? (Signal.) *The boat.*

- The next sentence also tells about the boat. What other word can we use to refer to **the boat?** (Signal.) *It.*
- So here's the next sentence: It had three sails.

5. Fill in the blanks. Start the second sentence in each item with **he, she** or **it.** Remember to start each sentence with a capital. Raise your hand when you're finished.
   (Observe students and give feedback.)

Teaching Notes

About the only problem that students have with these activities is keying off spurious words in the subject. In lesson 15, for instance, one of the items is: **His mother** liked to fix cars. _____ worked in a car shop.

Sometimes, students will key on the word **his** in the first sentence and write "He" at the beginning of the second sentence. The simplest correction for this kind of mistake is to act shocked. "His mother is a he? He has a man for a mother? Wow!"

If you use this kind of correction one time, you'll probably never have to use it again.

In lesson 25, students are introduced to a rule for using pronouns in a passage. The rule: If two sentences in a row name the same thing, you change the second sentence so that it names **he, she,** or **it.**

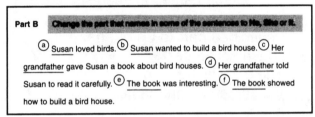

Part B Change the part that names in some of the sentences to He, She or It.

(a) Susan loved birds. (b) Susan wanted to build a bird house. (c) Her grandfather gave Susan a book about bird houses. (d) Her grandfather told Susan to read it carefully. (e) The book was interesting. (f) The book showed how to build a bird house.

You're going to change the part that names in some of the sentences to **he, she** or **it.**

2. I'll read the paragraph. Follow along. Susan loved birds. Susan wanted to build a bird house. Her grandfather gave Susan a book about bird houses. Her grandfather told Susan to read it carefully. The book was interesting. The book showed how to build a bird house.

3. Here's the rule for these sentences: If two sentences in a row name the same thing, we change the second sentence so it names **he, she** or **it.** Once more: If two sentences in a row name the same thing, we change the second sentence so it names **he, she** or **it.**

4. Sentence A names Susan. Look at sentence B. Everybody, who does sentence B name? (Signal.) *Susan.*
   • Two sentences in a row name the same person, so we change the second sentence to **he, she** or **it.** Which of those words refers to Susan? (Signal.) *She.*
   • Cross out **Susan** in sentence B. Write **she.** Remember to start with a capital. ✔
   • Here are the first and second sentences: Susan loved birds. **She** wanted to build a bird house.

5. Now we look at the next sentence. Everybody, who does sentence C name? (Signal.) *Her grandfather.*
   • Does that sentence name the same person sentence B names? (Signal.) *No.*
   • So we **don't** change sentence C. We don't have two sentences in a row that name the same person. Sentence B refers to **Susan.** Sentence C refers to **her grandfather.**

6. Look at the next sentence—sentence D. Everybody, who does sentence D name? (Signal.) *Her grandfather.*
   • Does that sentence name the same person sentence C names? (Signal.) *Yes.*

• So we have two sentences in a row that name the same person—sentence C and sentence D. Everybody, which sentence do you change? (Signal.) *Sentence D.*
• You change **her grandfather** in sentence D to **he, she** or **it.** Which word refers to **her grandfather?** (Signal.) *He.*
Change sentence D to **he.** ✔

7. Look at the next sentence—sentence E. Everybody, what does sentence E name? (Signal.) *The book.*
   • Does that sentence name the same thing sentence D names? (Signal.) *No.*
   • So we don't have to change sentence E. We don't have two sentences in a row that name the same thing.

8. Look at the last sentence—sentence F. Everybody, what does sentence F name? (Signal.) *The book.*
   • Does that sentence name the same thing sentence E names? (Signal.) *Yes.*
   • They both name the book. So we have two sentences in a row that name the same thing—sentence E and sentence F. Which sentence do you change? (Signal.) *Sentence F.*
   • You change **the book** in sentence F to **he, she** or **it.** Which word refers to **the book?** (Signal.) *It.*
   • Change sentence F to **it.** ✔

9. I'll read the fixed-up paragraph. Check your work. Susan loved birds. Capital **S, She** wanted to build a bird house. Her grandfather gave Susan a book about bird houses. Capital **H, He** told Susan to read it carefully. The book was interesting. Capital **I, It** showed how to build a bird house.

10. Fix up any mistakes you made in part B. (Observe students and give feedback.)

Teaching Notes

Most students will not have serious problems with this exercise if you follow the wording of the exercise carefully. Don't add extraneous words, rules, or observations.

Sometimes students don't understand that they are supposed to look at two sentences in a row. You can usually spot problems of not understanding by weak responses to the questions that you present in steps 4 through 8. If you get weak responses, direct students to touch the first part of each sentence you name. In step 4, you would say, "Sentence A names **Susan.** Touch that part of the sentence. With your other hand touch the underlined part of Sentence B." Then present the rest of the step as specified. Repeat the same procedure for the rest of the sentences.

Students work variations of the activity above in the following lessons. In lesson 32, they are introduced to a variation involving the pronoun **they.**

In lesson 51, a clarity rule is presented. The rule: If there are two men named in a sentence, you shouldn't begin the next sentence with **he.** If there are two women named in a sentence, you shouldn't begin the next sentence with **she.** Here's part of the activity from lesson 52 (the second time students have applied the rule).

Part A

1. Tom waved to Martha. ~~Martha~~ She was riding a horse.

2. Larry wanted to meet James. ~~Larry~~ He had a new bike.

3. Barbara gave her sister a rabbit. ~~Her sister~~ She loved rabbits.

4. Mr. Ross and Mr. Long were teachers. ~~Mr. Ross~~ He taught math.

5. Bill went fishing with Linda. ~~Linda~~ She caught four fish.

6. Ann and her mother went to a party. ~~Ann~~ She carried a cake.

- Remember the new rules for writing clearly: If there are two men in a sentence, you shouldn't begin the next sentence with **he.** If there are two women in a sentence, you shouldn't begin the next sentence with **she.**

2. I'll read the sentences in item 1: Tom waved to Martha. **Blank** was riding a horse. How many women are named in the first sentence? (Signal.) *One.*

- So should the next sentence begin with **she?** (Signal.) *Yes.*

- Cross out **Martha** at the beginning of the next sentence. ✔

- I'll read both sentences in item 1: Tom waved to Martha. She was riding a horse. We know who **she** refers to— Martha.

3. I'll read the sentences in item 2: Larry wanted to meet James. **Blank** had a new bike. How many men are in the first sentence? (Signal.) *Two.*

- Should we begin the next sentence with **he?** (Signal.) *No.*

- Cross out **he** at the beginning of the next sentence. ✔

- I'll read both sentences in item 2: Larry wanted to meet James. Larry had a new bike. Now the sentences give a clear picture about **who** had the new bike.

4. Do the rest of the items yourself. Read the first sentence. See if it names two men or two women. Figure out whether the next sentence will be clear if it starts with **he** or **she.** Cross out the word you don't use.
Raise your hand when you're finished.
(Observe students and give feedback.)

Teaching Notes

If students make more than occasional mistakes, read the item with the incorrect pronoun and point out the clarity problem.

For example: "Barbara gave her sister a rabbit. She loved rabbits. If I read that item, I wouldn't know whether Barbara loved rabbits or her sister loved rabbits."

For the other item type, point out that the pronoun is clear.

Bill went fishing with Linda. She caught four fish.

"Tell me the name of the person who caught the four fish."

"Yes, there's only one person who could be **she.**"

In lesson 55, students apply the clarity rule to sentences in a passage. For some sentences, the pronoun is appropriate. For others, the person's name is needed to assure clarity. Here's the exercise from lesson 55.

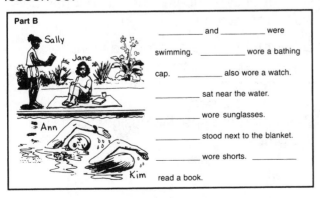

Part B

_____ and _____ were swimming. _____ wore a bathing cap. _____ also wore a watch.
_____ sat near the water.
_____ wore sunglasses.
_____ stood next to the blanket.
_____ wore shorts. _____ read a book.

- You've learned two rules about using the pronouns **he** or **she.** First, you learned that you must introduce a person with the person's name before you refer to that person with **he** or **she.** You also learned that if a sentence names two men or two women, the next sentence shouldn't begin with **he** or **she** because the sentence will be unclear. We won't know which **he** or **she** the sentence is telling about.
- We'll use those rules to figure out the words that go in each blank.
2. I'll read the first sentence: Blank and blank were swimming. Look at the picture. (Call on a student:) What words go in the blanks?
(Accept: *Ann and Kim* or *Kim and Ann.*)
- Here's the first sentence: **Ann** and **Kim** were swimming. Fill in the blanks for the first sentence. ✔
3. Listen: Ann and Kim were swimming. Here's the next sentence: Blank wore a bathing cap. Should we write **she** in the blank? (Signal.) *No.*
- Why not? (Call on a student. Idea: *There are two women in the first sentence.*)
- Everybody, who wore a bathing cap? (Signal.) *Ann.*
- Write **Ann** in the blank. ✔
- Here's the sentence: **Ann** wore a bathing cap.
4. Next sentence: Blank also wore a watch. Look at the picture and see if we're still talking about Ann. If we are, we can use the word **she.** Complete the sentence: Blank also wore a watch. Raise your hand when you're finished.
- Here's the sentence: **She** also wore a watch. Raise your hand if you got it right.

5. Next sentence: Blank sat near the water. Look at the picture and write the correct word in the blank. Raise your hand when you're finished.
   - Listen: Blank sat near the water. We're talking about a new person. So we must introduce that person. What word goes in the blank? (Signal.) *Jane.*
   - Yes, **Jane.** Here's that sentence: **Jane** sat near the water.
6. Fill in the blanks for the rest of the sentences. Remember, you can use the word **she** if it gives a clear picture. If it doesn't give a clear picture, you have to name the person. Raise your hand when you're finished.
   (Observe students and give feedback.)
7. Check your work. I'll read the whole paragraph.
   - **Ann** and **Kim** were swimming. **Ann** wore a bathing cap. **She** also wore a watch. **Jane** sat near the water. **She** wore sunglasses. **Sally** stood next to the blanket. **She** wore shorts. **She** read a book.
8. Raise your hand if you filled in all the blanks correctly.
   Great job.
   - Everybody else, fix up any mistakes you made in part B.

The exercises following lesson 55 provide practice with the pronouns **him, her, they,** and **them.**

Teaching Notes

A major purpose of the clarity exercise is to assure that students understand the basis for judging sentences confusing or unclear. What students learn about pronoun clarity is what they will be expected to apply to their own writing; however, students have much more trouble editing their own writing than they have editing what others write. Typically, they will have to be reminded of pronoun clarity many times when they write. The good news is that you'll be able to communicate with them. If they write: **Tom and Billy went swimming. He hated the water;** you can use the basic test of clarity. "Your first sentence says: **Tom and Billy went swimming.** How many boys are named? Your next sentence names **he.** Would the reader know which he that is? Fix up your second sentence."

PRONOUNS AS A PART OF SPEECH
The analysis of pronouns as a part of speech is not introduced until students have worked with pronouns in the context of writing and communicating clearly. The label **pronoun** is introduced after students have learned to identify verbs. Verbs are easy for students to identify because they are the first word or words of the predicate. Some pronouns are also easy to identify. Those are pronouns that appear as the subject of sentences. The subject has one word; that word is a pronoun.

Other pronouns are harder to identify. Those are pronouns in the predicate (him, her, it, them). Identification of these pronouns is aided by the rule that pronouns stand for more specific designations like **the girl.**

In the first part-of-speech exercise (lesson 54) students replace subjects with the appropriate pronouns.

In lesson 55, students circle the subject of sentences and then write **P** in front of every sentence that has a pronoun for a subject.

In lesson 58, students identify the part of speech for numbered words in sentences. The words are either verbs or pronouns.

After students have worked with clarity exercises involving pronouns in the predicate, students identify verbs and pronouns in sentences. Here's part of the exercise from lesson 61.

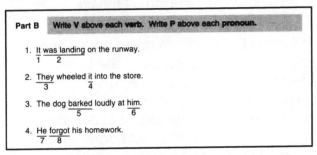

- You've learned two parts of speech. One part of speech is a **verb.** You've also learned another part of speech.
2. Listen: What part of speech are the words **he, she, it, they, him, her** and **them?** (Signal.) *Pronouns.* (Repeat step 2 until firm.)
3. Words in each sentence are underlined. You're going to tell the part of speech for words that are underlined.
4. First sentence: It was landing on the runway. The word **it** is underlined. What part of speech is **it?** (Signal.) *Pronoun.*
   - The words **was landing** are underlined. What part of speech are those words? (Signal.) *Verb.* (Repeat step 4 until firm.)
5. Write letters to show the part of speech for each number in part B. Write **V** above each verb. Write **P** above each pronoun. Raise your hand when you're finished. (Observe students and give feedback.)

NOUNS AS A PART OF SPEECH

Nouns are introduced after pronouns, starting in lesson 63. By the time students reach this lesson, they will have had a lot of practice using nouns in their writing. The basic writing exercise requires them to construct sentences that name and then tell more. To name, students use a proper noun or a class noun (the girls).

Nouns are introduced with a rule (nouns name persons, places, or things) and with the sentence-analysis rule: If the subject of a sentence is not a pronoun, the last word in the subject is a noun.

The sentence-analysis rule is very useful because it identifies nouns in a very tight way (with respect to the sentences the students will write and analyze). It also sets the stage for the last part of speech introduced in Level C—adjectives. The noun is the last word in the subject. The words that precede the noun are adjectives. Here's part of the exercise that introduces nouns (lesson 63).

Part D	Write the noun in each subject.

1. (A big dog) chased a cat.
2. (Girls) played outside my house.
3. (My best friend) was sick.
4. (That movie) ended early.
5. (James) fell asleep.

- The subject is circled in each sentence. None of the subjects are pronouns.
2. You're going to learn about a new part of speech. That part of speech is a **noun.** Here are the rules about nouns: Words that name persons, places or things are nouns. Once more: Words that name persons, places or things are nouns.
- Here's another rule about nouns: If the subject is not a pronoun, the last word in the subject is a noun.

3. Sentence 1: A big dog chased a cat. What's the subject? (Signal.) *A big dog.*
   - What's the last word in that subject? (Signal.) *Dog.*
   - So **dog** is a noun. What part of speech is **dog?** (Signal.) *Noun.*
   - Sentence 2: Girls played outside my house. What's the subject? (Signal.) *Girls.*
   - What's the last word in that subject? (Signal.) *Girls.*
     Right, that's the only word in the subject.
   - What part of speech is **girls?** (Signal.) *Noun.*
   - Sentence 3: My best friend was sick. What's the subject? (Signal.) *My best friend.*
   - What's the last word in that subject? (Signal.) *Friend.*
   - So **friend** is a noun. What part of speech is **friend?** (Signal.) *Noun.*
   - Sentence 4: That movie ended early. What's the subject? (Signal.) *That movie.*
   - What's the last word in that subject? (Signal.) *Movie.*
   - So **movie** is a noun. What part of speech is **movie?** (Signal.) *Noun.*
   - Sentence 5: James fell asleep. What's the subject? (Signal.) *James.*
   - What's the last word in that subject? (Signal.) *James.*
     Right, that's the only word in the subject.
   - What part of speech is **James?** (Signal.) *Noun.*
4. Your turn: For each sentence, write the noun that is in the subject. Raise your hand when you're finished.
   (Observe students and give feedback.)

Teaching Notes

Sentences 2 and 5 have one-word subjects. Some students may mistakenly call these words pronouns. To correct this mistake, say, **"Girls** is a noun. If it were a pronoun, it would be **they."**

or

"James is a noun. If it were a pronoun, it would be **he."**

If students make mistakes in step 3, repeat the tasks until the students are firm on responding to all the items.

In lesson 65, students relate nouns and pronouns. One purpose of the exercise is to show that pronouns are "more general" than nouns. That is, a pronoun can refer to more possible things than a class noun or proper noun can. Students draw lines connecting nouns to their appropriate pronoun referent.

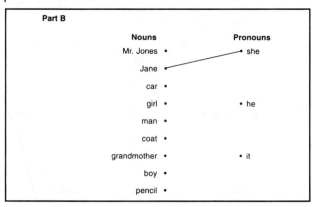

In lesson 68, students identify underlined words in sentences as **nouns, pronouns, or verbs.**

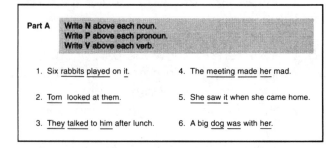

In lesson 71, students are presented with a test for identifying nouns in isolation. The test: If you can say the word **the** before the word in question and if the words name something, the word tested is a noun. If "the _____" does not name something, the word tested is not a noun.

This test is important because nouns appear in the predicate of sentences as well as in the subject. When they are in the subject, the rule about the last word of the subject guides identification of the noun. When nouns appear in the predicate, there is no handy rule for identifying them. (Students have worked with nouns in the subject, so they have learned something about the range of nouns before they are presented with the test for nouns.) Here's part of the exercise from lesson 71.

Part C	Write **N** in front of each noun.		
1. _____ girl	4. _____ us	7. _____ happy
2. _____ men	5. _____ yellow	8. _____ me
3. _____ they	6. _____ phone	9. _____ mud

You know that nouns name persons, places or things. Some nouns are easy. If you name a person—like Jerry, Linda or Doug—those names are nouns. They are the names of people. Places like Chicago, New York or California are easy. Those words name places, so those words are nouns. Some nouns are harder.

- I'll show you how to test them. I'll say **the** before different words. If I name something that makes sense, the word is a noun.

2. Listen: the apple. Did I name something? (Signal.) *Yes.*

- So **apple** is a noun. What part of speech is **apple?** (Signal.) *Noun.*
- Listen: the always. Did I name something? (Signal.) *No.*
- So **always** is not a noun.
- Listen: the sat. Did I name something? (Signal.) *No.*
- So **sat** is not a noun.

3. Listen: the dream. Did I name something? (Signal.) *Yes.*

- So what part of speech is **dream?** (Signal.) *Noun.*
- Listen: the meeting. Did I name something? (Signal.) *Yes.*
- So what part of speech is **meeting?** (Signal.) *Noun.*
- Listen: the little. Did I name something? (Signal.) *No.*
- So **little** is not a noun.
- Listen: the happy. Did I name something? (Signal.) *No.*
- So **happy** is not a noun.
(Repeat step 3 until firm.)

4. Find part C in your workbook. Some of these words are nouns. Test each word by saying **the** before the word. If you name something, the word is a noun.

5. Word 1 is **girl.** So you say **the girl.** Does that name something? (Signal.) *Yes.*

- So **girl** is a noun.
- Word 2 is **men.** What do you say to test that word? (Signal.) *The men.*
- Does that name something? (Signal.) *Yes.*
- So **men** is a noun.
- Word 3 is **they.** So what do you say? (Signal.) *The they.*
- Does that name something? (Signal.) *No.*
- So **they** is not a noun.
(Repeat step 5 until firm.)

6. Listen: Test each word by saying **the** before the word. Then write **N** in front of each word that's a noun. Don't write anything in front of the other words. Raise your hand when you're finished. (Observe students and give feedback.)

In lesson 73, students apply the test for nouns to nouns in the predicate.

Part A

1. She bought a new car.

2. They went to a crowded beach.

3. Sam cooked dinner for them.

4. My truck ran over it.

- You've learned that if the subject of a sentence is not a pronoun, the last word in the subject is a noun. You've also learned how to test words to see if they are nouns. You say **the** before the word. If you name something, the word is a noun.
- Every sentence in part A has a noun that's underlined. Some of the nouns are not in the subject. They're in the predicate.
2. Sentence 1: She bought a new car. The underlined words are **she, bought** and **car.** I'll test those words. You tell me if each word is a noun or not a noun.
- Listen: the she. Is **she** a noun? (Signal.) *No.*
- Listen: the bought. Is **bought** a noun? (Signal.) *No.*
- Listen: the car. Is **car** a noun? (Signal.) *Yes.*
3. Your turn: There is one underlined noun in each sentence. Write **N** over the underlined noun in each sentence. Don't do anything to the other underlined words. Raise your hand when you're finished.
(Observe students and give feedback.)
4. Check your work.
- Sentence 1. What's the noun? (Signal.) *Car.*
- Sentence 2. What's the noun? (Signal.) *Beach.*
- Sentence 3. What's the noun? (Signal.) *Sam.*
- Sentence 4. What's the noun? (Signal.) *Truck.*

5. The other underlined words in part A are either verbs or pronouns. Your turn: Write **P** above each pronoun and **V** above each verb. Raise your hand when you're finished. Remember, when you're finished, every underlined word should have a letter above it.
(Observe students and give feedback.)

ADJECTIVES AS A PART OF SPEECH
In Level C, students are not encouraged to use adjectives effusively when they write. The reason is that the initial goal of writing is clarity. For most of the writing activities, clarity is not improved with the addition of flowery adjectives.

Work on adjectives as a part of speech begins in lesson 91. Adjectives are the last part of speech taught in the level. The analysis of adjectives is based on the procedure of first finding the noun, then identifying words in front of the noun that tell about the noun. Those words are adjectives. This analysis permits students to identify words like **the** and **a** as adjectives (which is what they are). Words like **their, his,** and **my** are also adjectives. Here's the introduction from lesson 91.

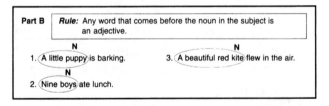

The subject of each sentence is circled. An **N** is written above the noun in each subject. You're going to learn about a new part of speech: **adjectives.**
- Here's the rule for these sentences: Any word that comes before the noun in the subject is an adjective. Once more: Any word that comes before the noun in the subject is an adjective.
2. Sentence 1: A little puppy is barking. What's the whole subject? (Signal.) *A little puppy.*
Yes, a little puppy.

- What's the noun? (Signal.) *Puppy.*
- Both the words that come before **puppy** are adjectives.
- What's the first adjective? (Signal.) *A.*
- What's the next adjective? (Signal.) *Little.*
  (Repeat step 2 until firm.)
3. Sentence 2: Nine boys ate lunch. What's the whole subject? (Signal.) *Nine boys.*
- What's the noun? (Signal.) *Boys.*
- How many adjectives are before the noun? (Signal.) *One.*
- Yes, one. What is it? (Signal.) *Nine.*
  (Repeat step 3 until firm.)
4. Sentence 3: A beautiful red kite flew in the air. What's the whole subject? (Signal.) *A beautiful red kite.*
- What's the noun? (Signal.) *Kite.*
- How many adjectives are before the noun? (Signal.) *Three.*
- What's the first adjective? (Signal.) *A.*
- What's the next adjective? (Signal.) *Beautiful.*
- What's the last adjective? (Signal.) *Red.*
  (Repeat step 4 until firm.)

Teaching Notes

Students should be quite firm on nouns in the subject before this lesson. The initial exercises deal with adjectives in the subject because students are less likely to have trouble identifying the nouns in the subject and because it's easier to identify the words that tell about the noun in the subject. When nouns are in the predicate (She went to the corner **store**), the test of whether a word tells about a **store** is not always clear to the students. Is the word **to** an adjective? They might reason this way: She went **to** the store, so **to** must tell something about the store.

Later exercises introduce the rule that adjectives tell **what kind** or **how many**. Here's the first part of the introduction from lesson 94.

1. You've learned about adjectives. Words that come before nouns are adjectives. Adjectives tell **what kind** or **how many**.
- Here's a noun: **shoes.** Here's that noun with an adjective that tells what kind of shoes: **big** shoes. Here's that noun with a different adjective: **new** shoes.
2. Your turn: Say **shoes** with a different adjective that tells **what kind.**
   (Call on several students. Praise responses such as: *Old shoes, small shoes, dirty shoes, blue shoes, etc.*)
3. Other adjectives tell **how many.** Here's the noun **shoes** with an adjective that tells **how many: two** shoes.
- Your turn: Say **shoes** with a different adjective that tells **how many.** (Call on several students. Praise responses such as: *Six shoes, many shoes, ten shoes, some shoes, etc.*)
4. Words like **a** or **the** are adjectives because they tell **how many. A** shoe is one shoe; **the** shoe is one shoe. Remember, an adjective tells **what kind** of noun or **how many**.

The final activities in the program are consolidation exercises in which students identify verbs, pronouns, nouns, and adjectives in sentences. The primary emphasis throughout the grammar track is on sentences because words have different parts of speech depending on their placement in sentences. In the sentence, "I went with her," the word **her** is a pronoun. In the sentence, "Her bike was red," **her** is an adjective.

At the end of Level C, students have a good beginning understanding of verbs, pronouns, nouns, and adjectives. Students are able to relate them to sentences. Students have a good understanding of subject and predicate—which is probably the most important aspect of the sentence analysis. With the base that they have at the end of Level C, they are ready to learn more about both grammar and punctuation.

Mechanics

In Level C, students learn basic rules for capitalizing and using ending marks. They learn rules for commas, quotes, and apostrophes.

CAPITALS AND ENDING MARKS

One of the more serious problems that students have when they write is writing in sentence units. Part of the problem comes from their lack of knowledge about what sentences are. Because they have trouble identifying the sentences they are trying to compose, they understandably have trouble putting capitals at the beginning of sentences and periods or question marks at the end.

The first work with capitals and periods begins in lesson 1. Students copy sentences or complete isolated sentences. For both activities they capitalize the first word and put a period at the end of each sentence.

Starting in lesson 17 (after students have learned the basic subject-predicate analysis for declarative sentences), the work on capitals and periods focuses more on identifying sentences in a passage. The first activity involves a paragraph that has no capitals and no periods. Students use the subject-predicate analysis to identify the sentences, then capitalize the first word and mark the end with a period.

A variation of this activity is presented in lesson 24. For this variation, some sentences lack capitals, some lack periods, and some are correct. Here's the student activity from lesson 24.

Part A	Put in the missing capitals and periods.

> every student in the class read a book Tom and Alice read a book about animals they learned about animals that live in different parts of the world Two students read a book about roses that book told how to take care of roses.

Teaching Notes

Remember, the purpose of this teaching is to help students when they write. If students write in non-sentences, take them through the basic steps for figuring out how to make their sentences mechanically correct. Ask, "What's the subject? . . . What's the predicate? . . . Now that you know the sentence, you can put in the capital at the beginning and the period at the end." (If the sentence the student writes is not a type that had been introduced in Level C, simply show the student where the capital and period go.)

In lesson 29, students are introduced to a rule about persons' names. The rule: Each part of a person's name begins with a capital. This rule helps students with otherwise complicated names such as "Mister Henry Jackson."

In lesson 85, students learn that names for days of the week and months of the year are always capitalized.

In lesson 97, students learn a general rule about persons or places. This rule covers a wide variety of applications. The rule: If the noun is the name of **one** person or **one** place, all parts of the name are capitalized. Here's the introduction to the rule.

1. You've learned that nouns name persons, places or things. Some nouns are always capitalized. Here's a rule about the names of persons or places: If the noun is the name of **one** person or **one** place, all parts of the name are capitalized.

2. **Sally** is capitalized because that name is supposed to name one person.

- Listen: Miss Sally Brown. All parts are capitalized, because that is the name of one person.
- Listen: the street. Nothing is capitalized, because **the street** could tell us about a lot of different places.
- Listen: Elm Street. All parts are capitalized, because that is the name of one place.

3. Listen: that park. Is anything capitalized? (Signal.) *No.*
- Listen: Stanley Park. Is anything capitalized? (Signal.) *Yes.*
- Yes, both parts of the name are capitalized.
  Listen: Atlantic Ocean. Is anything capitalized? (Signal.) *Yes.*
- Yes, both parts of the name are capitalized.
  Listen: that store. Is anything capitalized? (Signal.) *No.*
- Listen: Ace Grocery Store. Is anything capitalized? (Signal.) *Yes.*
- Yes, all parts of the name are capitalized.
- Listen: my doctor. Is anything capitalized? (Signal.) *No.*
- Listen: Doctor Jones. Is anything capitalized? (Signal.) *Yes.*
- Listen: Uncle Jake. Is anything capitalized? (Signal.) *Yes.*
- Yes, both parts of the name are capitalized.
  (Repeat step 3 until firm.)

4. Listen: Chicago, Illinois. Is anything capitalized? (Signal.) *Yes.*
- Chicago, Illinois is the name of one place, so both parts of the name are capitalized.
- Listen: (name students' city and state). Is anything capitalized? (Signal.) *Yes.*
- That's the name of one place, so both parts are capitalized.

APOSTROPHES

Work on apostrophes begins in lesson 44. Students are shown that the apostrophe is an indicator that something has been deleted. This rule is important because it has a counterpart with commas. Commas are sometimes used to indicate where conjunctions have been deleted.

In lessons 44 and 45, apostrophes in possessive words are introduced.

Part C	Write the missing word in each item.		
1. the hat that belongs to the boy	the	boy's	hat
2. the bone that belongs to the dog	the		bone
3. the car that belongs to her father	her		car
4. the arm that belongs to the girl	the		arm
5. the book that belongs to my friend	my		book
6. the toy that belongs to the cat	the		toy

- Some words tell that something belongs to something else. Those words have a punctuation mark called an apostrophe.

2. Touch item 1: the hat that belongs to the boy. Here's what we write: the **boy's** hat. We write the word **boy** and then put an apostrophe before the **s.**
- I'll spell **boy's:** *b-o-y*-apostrophe-*s.* Your turn: Spell **boy's.** (Signal.) *B-o-y-apostrophe-s.*
- Touch item 2: the bone that belongs to the dog. We write the **dog's** bone. I'll spell **dog's:** d-o-g-apostrophe-s. Your turn: Spell **dog's.** (Signal.) *D-o-g-apostrophe-s.*

3. Touch item 3: the car that belongs to her father. What do we write? (Signal.) *Her father's car.*
- Spell **father's.** (Signal.) *F-a-t-h-e-r-apostrophe-s.*
- Touch item 4: the arm that belongs to the girl. What do we write? (Signal.) *The girl's arm.*
- Spell **girl's.** (Signal.) *G-i-r-l-apostrophe-s.* (Repeat step 3 until firm.)
4. Your turn: Write the missing word in each item. Raise your hand when you're finished. (Observe students and give feedback.)
5. Check your work.
- Item 2: the dog's bone. Spell **dog's.** (Signal.) *D-o-g-apostrophe-s.*
- Item 3: her father's car. Spell **father's.** (Signal.) *F-a-t-h-e-r-apostrophe-s.*
- Item 4: the girl's arm. Spell **girl's.** (Signal.) *G-i-r-l-apostrophe-s.*
- Item 5: my friend's book. Spell **friend's.** (Signal.) *F-r-i-e-n-d-apostrophe-s.*
- Item 6: the cat's toy. Spell **cat's.** (Signal.) *C-a-t-apostrophe-s.*
6. Raise your hand if you made no mistakes. Great job.
- Everybody else, fix up any mistakes you made in part C.

Starting in lesson 46, students complete sentences with the appropriate possessive words. Here's the exercise from lesson 46.

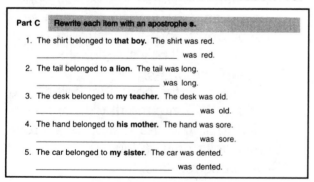

Part C   Rewrite each item with an apostrophe s.
1. The shirt belonged to **that boy.** The shirt was red.
_____ was red.
2. The tail belonged to **a lion.** The tail was long.
_____ was long.
3. The desk belonged to **my teacher.** The desk was old.
_____ was old.
4. The hand belonged to **his mother.** The hand was sore.
_____ was sore.
5. The car belonged to **my sister.** The car was dented.
_____ was dented.

1. Everybody, pencils down. Find part C.
- You're going to complete sentences that tell about something that belongs to something else.
2. Touch item 1.
The shirt belonged to that boy. The shirt was red.
Listen to the first sentence again: The shirt belonged to **that boy.** Who did the shirt belong to? (Signal.) *That boy.*
- So we write **that boy's shirt.** Spell **boy's.** (Signal.) *B-o-y-apostrophe-s.*
- Write **that boy's shirt.** Raise your hand when you're finished.
- Read the whole sentence you completed. (Signal.) *That boy's shirt was red.*
3. Touch item 2.
The tail belonged to **a lion.** The tail was long. Who did the tail belong to? (Signal.) *A lion.*
- So what do we write? (Signal.) *A lion's tail.* (Repeat step 3 until firm.)
4. Spell **lion's.** (Signal.) *L-i-o-n-apostrophe-s.*
- Write **a lion's tail.** Raise your hand when you're finished.
- Read the whole sentence you completed. (Signal.) *A lion's tail was long.*
5. Touch item 3.
The desk belonged to **my teacher.** The desk was old. Who did the desk belong to? (Signal.) *My teacher.*
- So what do we write? (Signal.) *My teacher's desk.*
- Fill in the blank. Raise your hand when you're finished.
- Read the whole sentence you completed. (Signal.) *My teacher's desk was old.*
- Spell **teacher's.** (Signal.) *T-e-a-c-h-e-r-apostrophe-s.*
6. Complete the rest of the items in part C. Just rewrite the first sentence for each item and you'll complete the new sentence. Raise your hand when you're finished. (Observe students and give feedback.)

Starting in lesson 49, students complete sentences that tell about a picture. They copy the first part of each sentence; then complete it, using the appropriate possessive word.

The final activity involving apostrophes requires students to discriminate between plural nouns and possessive nouns.

QUOTES

Students are taught to write the exact words that characters said. The sentence form that is taught in Level C begins by naming the person:

James said, "I'm ready."

or

She asked, "Will you go with us?"

Level C does not teach students to write sentences that have an "irregular" order: "When will we go?" he asked.

The introduction to direct quotes begins in lesson 53. Students write sentences from pictures that show somebody talking. Here's the first part of the work in lesson 53.

- In each picture, somebody said something. You're going to complete sentences that tell what they said.
2. Touch picture 1. Who said something in picture 1? (Signal.) *Stan.*
- What did Stan say? (Signal.) *My foot feels better.*
- Touch picture 2.
  Who said something in picture 2? (Signal.) *Miss Woods.*
- What did Miss Woods say? (Signal.) *I am hungry.*
- Touch picture 3.
  Who said something in picture 3? (Signal.) *A boy.*
- What did a boy say? (Signal.) *It is very late.*
3. My turn to say sentences that tell what the people said. Touch the picture of Stan.
- Listen: Stan said, "My foot feels better." Everybody, say that sentence. (Signal.) *Stan said, "My foot feels better."*
- Touch the picture of Miss Woods. Here's the sentence for that picture: Miss Woods said, "I am hungry." Everybody, say that sentence. (Signal.) *Miss Woods said, "I am hungry."*

- Touch the picture of a boy.
  Here's the sentence for that picture: A boy said, "It is very late." Everybody, say that sentence. (Signal.) *A boy said, "It is very late."*
  (Repeat step 3 until firm.)
4. I'll show you how to write those sentences. You write them with a **comma** and with **quote marks**.
- Everybody, touch the picture of Stan. Say the sentence for Stan. (Signal.) *Stan said, "My foot feels better."*
- (Write on the board:)

> **Stan said**

- Here's the first part of the sentence. Now I make a comma.
- (Add comma:)

> **Stan said,**

- That's a comma. Now I make quote marks to show that he's going to say something.
- (Make quote marks:)

> **Stan said, "**

- Now I write the exact words he said. Everybody, what are the words he said? (Signal.) *My foot feels better.*
  The first word he said is capitalized. (Signal.) *Watch.*
- (Write:)

> **Stan said, "My foot feels better**

- Now I end the sentence with a period.
- (Make a period at the end of the sentence:)

> **Stan said, "My foot feels better.**

- And I show that Stan stopped talking by ending with quote marks.
- (Make quote marks at the end of the sentence to show:)

> **Stan said, "My foot feels better."**

5. Copy this sentence. Remember, write **Stan said.** Then make a comma. Then make quote marks. Write the exact words Stan said, starting with a capital. Make another set of quote marks after the period at the end of the sentence. Raise your hand when you're finished. (Observe students and give feedback.)

Beginning in lesson 59, students write sentences that have a question in direct quotes. In lesson 61, students write a short paragraph about a picture. One of the sentences they write tells the exact words that a character said.

You're going to write a short paragraph about this picture.
2. You'll start your paragraph with the sentence that is already written. Touch that sentence. I'll read it: Each person caught three fish.

- In the picture, Mr. Smith is standing next to his fish and Jenny is standing next to her fish. You'll write a sentence that tells about Mr. Smith's fish. You'll write a sentence that tells about Jenny's fish. Then you'll write a sentence that tells what Jenny said. I'll say that sentence. Listen: Jenny said, "Thank you for showing me how to fish."

3. Write your paragraph. Start with the sentence that is already written. Then write a sentence about Mr. Smith's fish, a sentence about Jenny's fish, and a sentence about what Jenny said in the picture. Remember to punctuate that sentence with a comma and quote marks. Raise your hand when you're finished. You have 4 minutes. (Observe students and give feedback.)
4. (After 4 minutes, say:) Stop writing. (Call on several students to read their paragraphs.)
5. (Write on the board:)

> **She said, "Thank you for showing me how to fish."**

- Check your paragraph to make sure you correctly punctuated the sentence that tells what Jenny said. You could start the sentence with the words **she said** or **Jenny said.** Raise your hand if you punctuated that sentence correctly.
- Everybody else, fix up any mistakes.

In lesson 65, students write a single quote that contains two sentences. (The boy said, "Let's go home. I'm tired.")

In lesson 87, students learn a rule about paragraphing. The rule: Only one person can talk in a paragraph. If another person starts talking, you start a new paragraph.

The work on quotes continues to the end of the level. Students write passages in which they apply the rules they have learned about punctuating direct quotes and starting a new paragraph when a new person talks.

COMMAS

In Level C, students learn two rules for using commas (in addition to the comma used in direct-quote sentences). The first rule: If a sentence begins with part of the predicate, make a comma just before the subject.

The second rule: A comma replaces the word **and** in a series of phrases.

> **He bought carrots, lettuce and apples.**

(The **and** joining **carrots** and **lettuce** is omitted and replaced with a comma.)

The first comma rule is introduced in lesson 64. Students first circle the subject, underline the whole predicate, and make a line over the part that tells when. Then the comma rule is introduced. Here's that part of the activity.

> **Part A**
>
> 1. Jane walked home after school.
>   After school Jane walked home.
>
> 2. Tom read a book in the evening.
>   In the evening Tom read a book.
>
> 3. The girl rubbed her eyes when the lights came on.
>   When the lights came on the girl rubbed her eyes.

5. Here's a rule about punctuation: If a sentence begins with part of the predicate, you should have a comma just before the subject. That comma tells you that part of the predicate is in front of the subject. Listen again: If a sentence begins with part of the predicate, you should have a comma to show where the **subject** begins.
6. Touch the second sentence in item 1. After school, Jane walked home. That sentence begins with part of the predicate. Listen: Put a comma just before the subject begins. Put it just before the word **Jane.** ✔

- Touch the second sentence in item 2. In the evening, Tom read a book. That sentence begins with part of the predicate. So you need a comma just before the subject begins. What's the subject? (Signal.) *Tom.* Put a comma just before **Tom. ✔**
- The second sentence in item 3 says: When the lights came on, the girl rubbed her eyes. Fix up that sentence. Put a comma just before the subject begins. **✔**
- The subject is **the girl.** You should have put a comma before the word **the.** Raise your hand if you got it right.
- Everybody else, fix it up if you made a mistake.

In following lessons, students rewrite regular-order sentences so that they begin with the part of the predicate that tells when.

In lesson 73, students rewrite a paragraph so that some sentences begin with a part that tells when. All sentences in the original paragraph are in regular order.

After students have been taught about punctuating sentences that begin with a part that tells when (including the notion that these sentences have capitals only at the beginning, not another capital to mark the subject), students construct these sentences when they write their passages.

Students are taught to put a comma in sentences that begin with a part that tells when even if the part is short. Such punctuation helps students understand that punctuation is not completely arbitrary.

NOUN AND VERB PHRASES IN SERIES
Punctuating noun and verb phrases in a series starts in lesson 77. The punctuation rule is based on the idea that a regular-order sentence needs no special punctuation.

Ann had fun swimming <u>and</u> playing ball <u>and</u> digging in the sand.

No special punctuation is needed. When the word **and** is removed from the sentence, however, punctuation is needed to mark the places where the word **and** has been omitted. Here's the exercise from lesson 77.

Part B

> **Rule:** If you remove the word **and,** you must replace it with a comma.

1. Ann had fun swimming <u>and</u> playing ball and digging in the sand.
2. Girls <u>and</u> boys <u>and</u> dogs and cats slid down the hill.
3. James read a book and wrote two letters and called his uncle and cleaned his room.
4. A cat and a dog and a pig and a horse ran into the barn.

- Here's the rule about the word **and:** If you remove the word **and,** you must replace it with a comma. The comma shows that something is missing.
2. I'll read sentence 1: Ann had fun swimming and playing ball and digging in the sand. We don't need all the **ands.**
- Here's what we want the sentence to say: Ann had fun swimming, playing ball and digging in the sand.
- Everybody, cross out the underlined **and.** Replace it with a comma. Raise your hand when you're finished. (Observe students and give feedback.)
- (Call on a student:) Read your fixed-up sentence. Say **comma** where you wrote a comma.
  Ann had fun swimming, comma, playing ball and digging in the sand.
3. Sentence 2: Girls and boys and dogs and cats slid down the hill. We don't want so many **ands.**
- Cross out the underlined **ands.** Replace them with commas. Raise your hand when you're finished. (Observe students and give feedback.)
- (Call on a student:) Read your fixed-up sentence. Say **comma** where you wrote a comma.
  Girls, comma, boys, comma, dogs and cats slid down the hill.

4. Everybody, fix up sentence 3. Leave the last **and.** Replace the other **ands** with commas. Raise your hand when you're finished.
   (Observe students and give feedback.)
   • (Call on a student:) Read your fixed-up sentence. Say **comma** where you wrote a comma.
   James read a book, comma, wrote two letters, comma, called his uncle and cleaned his room.

5. Everybody, fix up sentence 4. Leave the last **and.** Replace the other **ands** with commas. Raise your hand when you're finished.
   (Observe students and give feedback.)
   • (Call on a student:) Read your fixed-up sentence. Say **comma** where you wrote a comma.
   A cat, comma, a dog, comma, a pig and a horse ran into the barn.

6. Raise your hand if you punctuated all the sentences correctly.
   • Everybody else, fix up any mistakes you made in part B.

In subsequent exercises, the word **and** is not underlined.

After students have learned the comma convention, they are introduced to application exercises that require them to construct sentences. Here's the activity from lesson 86.

Part C

1. Make up a sentence that tells who **went into the store.**
2. Make up a sentence that tells which animals **stood on a diving board.**
3. Make up a sentence that tells the things **the woman juggled.**

• You're going to write sentences that need a comma because you'll leave out the word **and.**

2. I'll read item 1: Make up a sentence that tells who went into the store.
   • (Call on a student:) Name the three people who went into the store in picture 1. (Idea: *Ted, Doris and Kim.*)
   • Yes, Ted, Doris and Kim went into the store. Everybody, write your sentence for picture 1. Raise your hand when you're finished.
   (Observe students and give feedback.)
   • (Call on several students to read their sentence. Praise sentences that name all three people and have the word **and** only before the last person.)

3. I'll read item 2: Make up a sentence that tells which animals stood on a diving board.
   • (Call on a student:) Name the three animals that stood on the diving board. (Idea: *A dog, a cat and a goat.*)
   • Everybody, write your sentence for picture 2. Raise your hand when you're finished.
   (Observe students and give feedback.)
   • (Call on several students to read their sentence. Praise sentences that name all three animals and have the word **and** only before the last animal.)

4. I'll read item 3: Make up a sentence that tells the things the woman juggled.
   • (Call on a student:) Name the three things the woman juggled.
   (Idea: *A bottle, a can and a ball.*)
   • Everybody, write your sentence for picture 3. Raise your hand when you're finished.
   (Observe students and give feedback.)
   • (Call on several students to read their sentence. Praise sentences that name all three items and have the word **and** only before the last object.)

5. Check your sentences. Make sure you have a comma where the word **and** could have gone.

6. Raise your hand if you got all the items right. Great job.
   • Everybody else, fix up any mistakes you made in part C.

Following work similar to that in lesson 86, students are required to write passages that contain sentences with omitted commas.

Throughout the work on mechanics, the emphasis moves from teaching a skill or applying a convention to writing.

Editing

Part of the transition from skill learning to writing is editing. Each skill or convention is first taught as a relatively simple rule or procedure. Next, students **edit** passages for violations of the "rule" that had been taught. The violations that are presented are typically mistakes that naive writers make. Finally, students apply the rule in their own writing.

Editing activities begin in lesson 30 and continue to the end of Level C. Editing activities appear in 56 lessons. The 56 activities present many of the mistakes that students make when they write. Editing the mistakes written by somebody else is far easier for students than dealing with mistakes in their own writing. The repeated practice in editing mistakes of others makes it easier for students to read and edit their own work.

Here's an early editing activity (lesson 37) in which students edit for sentences that begin with **And** or **And then.**

> **Part B**
>
> Sandra went to the zoo yesterday. And then she met her
>
> friends near the monkey house. And the monkeys were doing
>
> tricks. Two monkeys were swinging by their tails. And one monkey
>
> was doing flips. And then Sandra and her friends went to the snack
>
> bar. And they bought peanuts for the monkeys.

Here's a later editing activity (lesson 88). This editing activity reviews the various skills and conventions the students have been taught. The number at the end of each item indicates the number of mistakes. The mistakes have to do with possessives, verb agreement, capitalization, commas, sentence fragments, and ending marks.

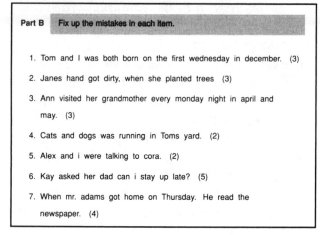

Part B   Fix up the mistakes in each item.

1. Tom and I was both born on the first wednesday in december. (3)
2. Janes hand got dirty, when she planted trees (3)
3. Ann visited her grandmother every monday night in april and may. (3)
4. Cats and dogs was running in Toms yard. (2)
5. Alex and i were talking to cora. (2)
6. Kay asked her dad can i stay up late? (5)
7. When mr. adams got home on Thursday. He read the newspaper. (4)

Reporting

Nearly all writing assignments in Level C are referenced to pictures. Students **report** on what a picture shows. The sentences they write have a past-tense verb. Accompanying the later writing exercises are checks. The checks indicate the major criteria the writing should achieve. The checks vary from assignment to assignment. Also, they become more "inclusive" as students progress through the program. Earlier checks are specific, such as, "Does each sentence begin with a capital and end with a period?" A check later in the program would be, "Are all your sentences written correctly?" This check implies checking the sentence for various mechanical criteria and logical details.

The first reporting exercises teach the discrimination between **reporting** and **inferring.** Here's the first part of the exercise from lesson 1.

Part A

Circle **reports** if a sentence reports on what the picture shows.
Circle **does not report** if the sentence does not report on what the picture shows.

1. The three men were brothers.	reports	does not report
2. Three men fished from a boat.	reports	does not report
3. The men were going to have fish for dinner.	reports	does not report
4. A big dog stood in the boat.	reports	does not report
5. All the men wore hats.	reports	does not report
6. One man held a net.	reports	does not report
7. One fishing pole bent down toward the water.	reports	does not report
8. A large fish was on the end of the line.	reports	does not report

1. This language program is going to teach you a lot about writing clearly. To write clearly, you have to think clearly and be smart. So you'll learn a lot about being smart. You'll also learn about the different rules you have to follow when you write. We'll do the first lesson today. The activities we'll work on are in your workbook.

2. Everybody, open your workbook to lesson 1. ✔
Look at the picture in part A.
You're going to learn about sentences that report on the picture.
Listen: If a sentence tells about something that you can touch in the picture, the sentence **reports** on the picture. If the sentence does not tell about something you can touch, the sentence **does not report.**
Once more: If the sentence tells you about something you can touch in the picture, the sentence **reports.**

3. Listen: One man was standing in the boat. That sentence reports. Touch the part of the picture that shows: One man was standing in the boat. ✔

• Listen: One woman was standing in the boat. Everybody, does that sentence report? (Signal.) *No.*
Right, nothing in the picture shows a woman standing in the boat.

4. Listen: Three dogs were swimming next to the boat. Everybody, does that sentence report? (Signal.) *No.*

• Listen: Two men were sitting in the boat. Everybody, does that sentence report? (Signal.) *Yes.*
Touch the part of the picture that shows two men sitting in the boat. ✔

• Listen: All the men wore hats. Everybody, does that sentence report? (Signal.) *Yes.*

• Listen: Two of the men were hungry. Everybody, does that sentence report? (Signal.) *No.*

• Listen: The men were going to have fish for dinner. This is tricky. Everybody, does that sentence report? (Signal.) *No.*

• It doesn't report because the picture doesn't **show** what they will have for dinner or even if they'll catch any fish. Maybe that man standing up in the boat is catching a turtle or an old tire.

5. Everybody, touch sentence 1 below the picture. Sentence 1.
I'll read sentence 1: The three men were brothers. Everybody, does that sentence report? (Signal.) *No.*

• The sentence does not report, so circle the words **does not report.** Find the words **does not report** on the same line as sentence 1. Then make a circle around those words. ✔

6. Everybody, touch sentence 2.
I'll read sentence 2: Three men fished from a boat. Everybody, does that sentence report? (Signal.) *Yes.*

• The sentence reports, so circle the word reports on the same line as sentence 2. Find the word **reports** and circle it. ✔

Beginning in lesson 6, students select sentences that tell the main thing illustrated characters did. This exercise is important because, when students "report" by naming a character and telling what the character did, they are expected to describe the **main thing** the character did.

Part E | For each picture, copy the sentence that tells the main thing the person did.

1. Mary

Mary held a glass.
Mary drank a glass of water.
Mary wore a belt.

2. Jill

Jill bent her leg.
Jill held the board with one hand.
Jill sawed a board.

2. Touch picture 1.
   One of the sentences next to the picture tells the main thing the person did. The other sentences tell about a detail.
   • First sentence: Mary held a glass. Say that sentence. (Signal.) *Mary held a glass.*
   • My turn: That's not the **main thing** Mary did. That's a **detail.**

• Next sentence: Mary drank a glass of water. Say that sentence. (Signal.) *Mary drank a glass of water.*
• That's the **main thing** Mary did.
• Next sentence: Mary wore a belt. Say that sentence. (Signal.) *Mary wore a belt.*
• Everybody, is that the **main thing** Mary did or **a detail?** (Signal.) *A detail.*

3. Touch picture 2.
   One of these sentences tells the **main thing** the person did. The other sentences tell about **a detail.**

4. First sentence: Jill bent her leg. Say that sentence. (Signal.) *Jill bent her leg.*
   • Everybody, is that the **main thing** Jill did or **a detail?** (Signal.) *A detail.*
   • Next sentence: Jill held the board with one hand. Say that sentence. (Signal.) *Jill held the board with one hand.*
   • Everybody, is that the main thing Jill did or a detail? (Signal.) *A detail.*
   • Next sentence: Jill sawed a board. Say that sentence. (Signal.) *Jill sawed a board.*
   • Everybody, is that the main thing Jill did or a detail? (Signal.) *The main thing.*
   (Repeat step 4 until firm.)

5. I'll read the instructions for part E: For each picture, copy the sentence that tells the main thing the person did. Don't copy any of the other sentences. You have one and a half minutes. Raise your hand when you're finished.
   (Observe students and give feedback.)

Starting in lesson 9, students compose sentences that tell the main thing characters did. This exercise is the first in which students check their work for various criteria.

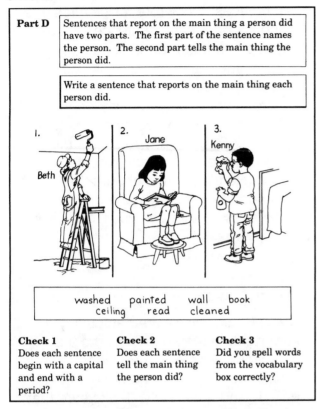

Part D | Sentences that report on the main thing a person did have two parts. The first part of the sentence names the person. The second part tells the main thing the person did.

Write a sentence that reports on the main thing each person did.

1. Beth
2. Jane
3. Kenny

washed   painted   wall   book
ceiling   read   cleaned

Check 1
Does each sentence begin with a capital and end with a period?

Check 2
Does each sentence tell the main thing the person did?

Check 3
Did you spell words from the vocabulary box correctly?

2. The rule in the box for part D tells about sentences that report on the main thing a person did. Touch that rule. I'll read: Sentences that report on the main thing a person did have two parts. The first part of the sentence **names the person.** The second part **tells the main thing the person did.**
Remember, the first part names; the second part tells more.

3. You're going to say sentences that report on the main thing each person did. Remember, when you report, you can only tell what the picture shows.
• Everybody, touch picture 1.
Name the person in that picture. (Signal.) *Beth.*

• Get ready to say a sentence that reports on the main thing Beth **did.** Don't say what Beth **is doing** or **was doing.** Start by naming Beth. Then tell the main thing Beth **did.** (Call on a student. Praise sentences such as: *Beth painted the ceiling.*)

4. Everybody, touch picture 2.
Name that person. (Signal.) *Jane.*
• Get ready to say a sentence that reports on the main thing Jane did. Don't say what Jane **is doing** or **was doing.** Make up a sentence that tells the main thing Jane **did.** (Call on a student. Praise sentences such as: *Jane read a book.*)

5. Touch the words in the vocabulary box as I read them: washed, painted, wall, book, ceiling, read, cleaned. Be sure to spell those words correctly if you use them.

6. I'll read the instructions for part D. Write a sentence that reports on the main thing each person did.
• Next to number 1 on your paper, write a sentence that reports on what the person in picture 1 did. Do the same thing for pictures 2 and 3. Be sure each sentence starts with a capital and ends with a period. You have 3 minutes. Raise your hand when you're finished. (Observe students and give feedback.)

7. (After 3 minutes, say:) Stop writing. If you didn't finish, you can write the rest of the sentences at the end of the lesson.
• (Write on the board:)

1 ☐   2 ☐   3 ☐

• Let's check your work. These are check boxes. Make boxes like these below your last sentence.
(Observe students and give feedback.)

8. Everybody, touch the box for check 1.
   - Here's check 1: Does each sentence begin with a capital and end with a period?
   - Read your sentences. If they begin with a capital and end with a period, put a check mark like this in box 1 on your paper. (Make a check mark in box 1.)
   - If you forgot any capitals or periods, fix up your sentences now and then make the check mark. Don't make a check mark until you've checked your sentences and fixed up any mistakes. Raise your hand when you're finished. (Observe students and give feedback.)
9. Now touch the box for check 2 on your paper.
   - Here's check 2: Does each sentence tell the main thing the person did?
   - Read over your sentences carefully. Each sentence should start out by naming the person. Then it should tell the main thing the person did. When all your sentences name and tell the main thing the person did, put a check mark in box 2. Raise your hand when you're finished. (Observe students and give feedback.)
10. Now touch the box for check 3.
    - Here's that check: Did you spell words from the vocabulary box correctly?
    - Look at each sentence. Make sure vocabulary words are spelled correctly. Fix up any mistakes and make a check mark in box 3. Raise your hand when you're finished. (Observe students and give feedback.)

11. I'll call on students to read their sentences. Listen to each sentence and see if it **names** the right person and tells **the main thing** that person **did.** (Call on individual students to read the sentences they wrote for pictures 1, 2 and 3. After each sentence, ask the group:) Is that a good sentence?
12. Raise your hand if you think you'll get a **super** paper.
    - I'll read your sentences later and hand them back at the beginning of the next lesson. I'll mark any mistakes I find.
    - Also on the next lesson, you'll have a test. Here's the rule about the test: If you don't make any more than 2 mistakes on the test, you'll get a **super** on your test.

Teaching Notes

Steps 6 through 12 are particularly important. In step 6, make sure that you circulate among the students. Praise the students who are working quickly and accurately. Make sure that others can hear your comments. If students are working slowly, warn them that they don't have unlimited time. "In about one more minute, you'll have to stop writing, so try to finish up."

When you tell students to stop writing (step 7), make sure they stop writing.

The general rules for conducting the checks and making them important to the students and effective for instruction are detailed on page 25 of the guide. Follow these procedures (or a variation of them) starting with lesson 9.

After directing each check, circulate among the students and see if they are following the check procedure. Do not "mother hen" them if you observe a mistake. If a student has a check mark in box one but has a mistake, tell the student, "You didn't fix up all your sentences so that they begin with a capital and end with a period. Read your sentences over very carefully. Find the sentence that's wrong and fix it up."

Remember, the more you show the students the mistakes they made and show them how to fix them up, the less some of them will listen to you when you're trying to instruct them.

Also, keep the checks moving fast. When the students have had a reasonable amount of time for check one (half a minute), present check two, or present the "random test" procedure described on page 25 for determining the points the group receives.

Remember, the checks teach the students a great deal about writing. If the checks are done effectively, students will actually do them. If not, some will fake it.

Starting in lesson 19, students work on a paragraph. The first sentence is written. That sentence tells the main thing a group of people did. Students then write a sentence for each illustrated character. These sentences tell the main thing each character did.

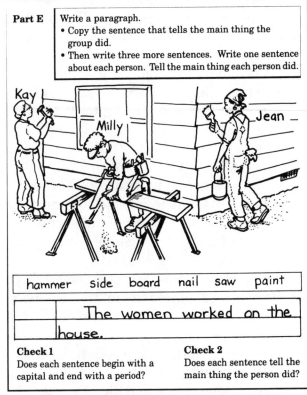

Part E

Write a paragraph.
• Copy the sentence that tells the main thing the group did.
• Then write three more sentences. Write one sentence about each person. Tell the main thing each person did.

hammer   side   board   nail   saw   paint

The women worked on the house.

Check 1
Does each sentence begin with a capital and end with a period?

Check 2
Does each sentence tell the main thing the person did?

2. Everybody, touch the words in the vocabulary box as I read them: hammer, side, board, nail, saw, paint. Be sure to spell those words correctly if you use them.

3. I'll read the instructions: Write a paragraph. Copy the sentence that tells the main thing the group did. Then write three more sentences. Write one sentence about each person. Tell the main thing each person did.

4. The sentence that tells the main thing the group did is written under the picture.
Everybody, read that sentence. (Signal.)
The women worked on the house.

• Everybody, copy that sentence. Remember to indent. Raise your hand when you're finished.
(Observe students and give feedback.)

5. Now you're going to write a sentence about each of the women. Touch Kay.

• Listen: Write a sentence that names Kay and tells the main thing she did. Start that sentence right after the period of the first sentence. Raise your hand when you're finished.

6. Touch Milly in the picture.

• Write a sentence that names Milly and tells the main thing she did. Remember to start that sentence right after the period of the last sentence. Raise your hand when you're finished.
(Observe students and give feedback.)

7. Now write a sentence that names Jean and tells the main thing she did. Remember to start that sentence right after the period. Raise your hand when you're finished.
(Observe students and give feedback.)

8. I'm going to call on several students to read their paragraph. Let's see who the good listeners are. Each paragraph starts with the sentence about the group. Then it should have a sentence about Kay, a sentence about Milly, and a sentence about Jean. Each of these sentences should tell the main thing that person did.

• If you hear a mistake, raise your hand. If a sentence is missing, raise your hand. If a sentence doesn't tell the main thing one of the women did, raise your hand. Listen carefully.

9. (Call on a student:) Read your paragraph. When you read it, stop at the end of each sentence so everybody can think about whether that sentence is right.

(Praise the paragraph if it has no mistakes.)

(To correct:)
(For each mistake that is identified, call on a student to tell how the sentence should be changed. Praise students for finding mistakes.)
a. (After each mistake is identified, say:) What should that sentence say?
(Call on a student with hand raised.)
b. (After each paragraph with no mistakes, say:) Everybody, was that a good paragraph?

10. (Call on several other students to read their paragraph. Praise good paragraphs.)

11. You're going to fix up your paragraph before you hand it in. Make 2 check boxes under your paragraph.

12. Here's check 1: Does each sentence begin with a capital and end with a period? Read each sentence you wrote and fix up any mistakes. Then make a check in box 1. Raise your hand when you're finished with check 1.
(Observe students and give feedback.)

13. Here's check 2: Does each sentence tell the main thing the person did? Make sure you have a sentence for each person and it tells the main thing the person did. Then make a check in box 2. Raise your hand when you're finished with check 2.
(Observe students and give feedback.)

14. Raise your hand if you think you'll get a **super** paper.
We'll see next time.

Teaching Notes

Follow the procedures in step 9 very closely. Enforce the idea that the reader is to stop at the end of each sentence. Don't accept poorly worded sentences. If a student reads, "Milly held a saw," prompt the group to identify the problem. (The sentence doesn't tell the main thing Milly did.)

Following each error, use the correction procedure in the shaded box. Praise students that have acceptable sentences.

Beginning in lesson 28, students write a paragraph about a group. They first write a sentence that tells the main thing the **group** did. Then they write two sentences about each member of the group. The first sentence tells the main thing the **character** did. The second sentence tells something else about that character. Here's the first part of the activity.

Part F	Write a paragraph that reports on the picture.
	• Begin with a good sentence that tells what the painters did.
	• Then write two sentences about each person. The first sentence should tell the main thing the person did.
	The second sentence should tell something else about the person.

room   ceiling   painted   bottom   roller
kneeled   knees   brushed   ladder   used

Check 1
Does each sentence begin with a capital and end with a period?

Check 2
Did you write two sentences about each person?

Check 3
Does the second sentence about each person begin with **he** or **she**?

• I'll read the instructions: Write a paragraph that reports on the picture. Begin with a good sentence that tells what the painters did. Then write two sentences about each person. The first sentence should tell the main thing the person did. The second sentence should tell something else about the person.

2. Touch the words in the vocabulary box as I read them: room, ceiling, painted, bottom, roller, kneeled, knees, brushed, ladder, used. Be sure to spell those words correctly if you use them.

3. Write a good sentence that tells the main thing the painters did. Raise your hand when you're finished.
(Observe students and give feedback.)

• (Call on several students to read their sentence. Praise sentences such as: *The painters painted the room.*)

4. Now write two sentences about Jim. Remember, the first sentence names Jim. The second sentence starts with **he.** Raise your hand when you're finished.
(Observe students and give feedback.)

• (Call on several students to read their sentences about Jim. Praise sentences that are consistent with the picture.)

5. Everybody, now you're going to write two sentences about Susan. What word will the second sentence about Susan start with? (Signal.) *She.*

• Write your sentences about Susan. Raise your hand when you're finished.
(Observe students and give feedback.)

Teaching Notes

Some of the second sentences may be a little stilted but acceptable. Others are not acceptable. These second sentences for Jim would be acceptable:

He used a paint brush.
He kneeled on newspapers.

Here are second sentences that are unacceptable because they refer to details that are irrelevant or redundant:

He wore shoes.
He looked at the wall.
He used paint.

In lesson 36, students write a paragraph about a series of pictures.

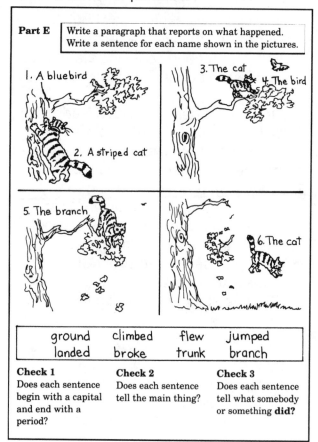

Part E | Write a paragraph that reports on what happened. Write a sentence for each name shown in the pictures.

1. A bluebird
2. A striped cat
3. The cat   4. The bird
5. The branch   6. The cat

| ground | climbed | flew | jumped |
| landed | broke | trunk | branch |

Check 1
Does each sentence begin with a capital and end with a period?

Check 2
Does each sentence tell the main thing?

Check 3
Does each sentence tell what somebody or something **did?**

I'll read the instructions: Write a paragraph that reports on what happened. Write a sentence for each name shown in the pictures.

2. Touch the words in the vocabulary box as I read them: ground, climbed, flew, jumped, landed, broke, trunk, branch.
3. Touch number 1 in the first picture. Name that animal. (Signal.) *A bluebird.*
• Write a sentence that tells the main thing a bluebird did in the picture. This sentence is the first one in your paragraph, so be sure to indent. Raise your hand when you're finished. (Observe students and give feedback.)
• (Call on several students to read their sentences. Praise sentences such as: *A bluebird stood on a branch.*)
4. Touch number 2. Name that animal. (Signal.) *A striped cat.*
• Write a sentence that tells the main thing a striped cat did in the picture. Don't write any numbers. Start writing the sentence about the striped cat just after the period. Give a clear picture of what the striped cat did in the first picture. Raise your hand when you're finished. (Observe students and give feedback.)
• (Call on several students to read their sentences. Praise sentences such as: *A striped cat climbed up the tree trunk.*)
5. Touch number 3. Name that animal. (Signal.) *The cat.*
• Write a sentence that tells the main thing the cat did in that picture. Raise your hand when you're finished. (Observe students and give feedback.)
• (Call on several students to read their sentences. Praise sentences such as: *The cat walked out on a branch.*)
6. Touch number 4. Name that animal. (Signal.) *The bird.*
• Finish your paragraph. Write a clear sentence for each of the names in the pictures. You'll write sentences for names 4, 5 and 6. Raise your hand when you're finished. (Observe students and give feedback.)

7. I'm going to call on several students to read their paragraphs. Listen carefully. Make sure each sentence tells the main thing. Make sure no sentences are missing. And make sure each sentence tells what somebody or something did. Raise your hand if you hear a mistake.

- (Call on several students to read their paragraphs. Praise good paragraphs.)

8. Now you're going to check your paragraph. Make 3 check boxes under your paragraph.

9. Check 1: Does each sentence begin with a capital and end with a period? Check your paragraph. Fix up any mistakes. Then make a check in box 1. Raise your hand when you're finished.

10. Check 2: Does each sentence tell the main thing? Read your paragraph. Make sure each sentence tells the main thing. Fix up any mistakes. Then make a check in box 2. Raise your hand when you're finished.

11. Check 3: Does each sentence tell what somebody or something **did?** Remember, you can't tell what somebody or something was doing. You have to tell what they did. Fix up any mistakes. Then make a check in box 3. Raise your hand when you're finished.

12. Next time, I'll read some of the **super** paragraphs to you.

Teaching Notes

Students are not to write numbers when they write the paragraph. The numbers are guides to the order of the sentences.

As students learn new skills, the assignments for story writing become more elaborate. After students have learned to write sentences that contain direct quotes, students write passages that include direct quotes.

Inferring

After students have practiced reporting on what pictures show, they are introduced to inferences. All the inferences they will draw are **necessary** inferences. These inferences are based on the differences between two pictures. If the cat is on the table in one picture and on the windowsill in the next picture, the cat must have moved from the table to the windowsill. The difference between the pictures may not suggest whether the cat moved quickly or slowly or even whether the cat received assistance, but the difference implies that the cat moved. Inferences of this type are very important because they force the writer to provide details that make the passage they write easy to understand. Without them, the passage lacks important information.

The first inferring activity appears in lesson 47. Students write sentences about a blank picture.

Part C Write three sentences that tell what must have happened in the middle picture. Tell about **the candle, the newspapers and the woman.**

1.   2.   3.

bucket   fell   burn

- You've **reported** on what pictures show, but you can't always report. Sometimes you have to be smart and figure out what must have happened. The pictures in part C are supposed to show what happened first and next and next, but the middle picture is missing.

2. Let's see if you can figure out what must have happened in the middle picture. We start with picture 1.
   - (Call on a student:) What did the cat do in that picture? (Idea: *Jumped onto a shelf.*)
   - Who can tell about the candle in that picture? (Call on a student. Idea: *The candle fell off the shelf.*)
   - Now go to picture 3. (Call on a student:) Where's the candle in picture 3? (Idea: *On the newspapers.*)
   - (Call on a student:) What's burning in that picture? *The newspapers.*

3. Here's the first part of the story: A woman was looking out the window. Her cat jumped onto a shelf. The cat knocked over a burning candle that was on the shelf.

4. Now you'll tell me what must have happened in the middle picture. You'll tell about the candle, the newspapers and the woman. Listen: Make up a sentence about the candle. (Call on a student. Praise sentences such as: *The candle landed on the newspapers.*)
   - Now make up a sentence that tells what the newspapers did. (Call on a student. Praise sentences such as: *The newspapers started to burn.*)
   - Now make up a sentence that tells what the woman must have done in the middle picture. Be careful. Don't tell what she did in the last picture. Tell what she must have done in the middle picture. (Call on a student. Praise sentences such as: *The woman picked up a bucket of water.*)

5. I'll read the words in the vocabulary box: bucket, fell, burn.

6. Your turn: Write a paragraph. Write three sentences that tell what must have happened in the middle picture. Tell about the candle, the newspapers and the woman. Raise your hand when you're finished.
   (Observe students and give feedback.)

7. I'll call on different students to read their paragraph.
   - (Call on several students. Praise sentences such as: *The candle landed on the newspapers. The newspapers started to burn. The woman picked up a bucket of water.*)

In lesson 51, students write about the missing picture and the last picture. Here's the student material from lesson 51.

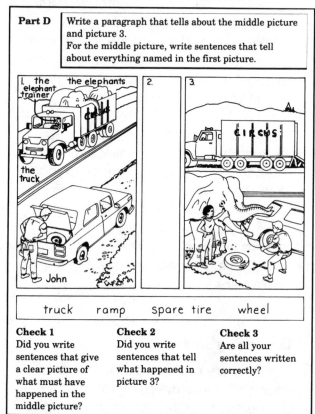

Beginning in lesson 63, students write about the first picture and the missing picture. They write the exact words a character says. Here's the exercise from lesson 63.

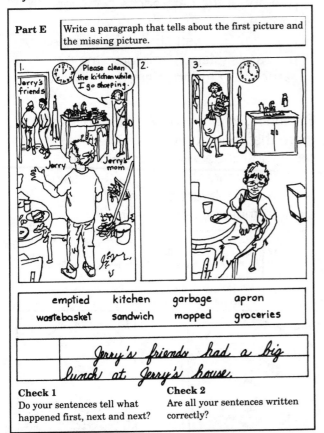

| Part E | Write a paragraph that tells about the first picture and the missing picture. |

emptied   kitchen   garbage   apron
wastebasket   sandwich   mopped   groceries

Jerry's friends had a big lunch at Jerry's house.

Check 1
Do your sentences tell what happened first, next and next?

Check 2
Are all your sentences written correctly?

- You're going to write a paragraph that tells about the first picture and the missing picture.
- I'll read the words in the vocabulary box: emptied, kitchen, garbage, apron, wastebasket, sandwich, mopped, groceries.
- You'll start your paragraph with the sentence that is already written. Touch that sentence. I'll read it: Jerry's friends had a big lunch at Jerry's house.

2. You'll write sentences about the first picture. The first sentences will tell the main thing the people in the first picture did. Who can make up a sentence that tells what Jerry's friends did?
- (Call on a student. Idea: *Jerry's friends walked out the back door.*)
  The next sentence will tell what Jerry did.

- (Call on a student. Idea: *Jerry waved good-bye to his friends.*)
  The next sentence will tell what Jerry's mother did.
- (Call on a student. Idea: *Jerry's mother opened the kitchen door.*)
- The next sentence will tell what Jerry's mother said. Everybody, what did Jerry's mother say? (Signal.) *Please clean the kitchen while I go shopping.*
- Write the first part of your paragraph. Copy the first sentence. Then tell about the first picture. Write sentences that tell what Jerry's friends did, what Jerry did and what Jerry's mother did. Then write what she said. Remember to punctuate that sentence with a comma and quote marks. Raise your hand when you've finished that part of your paragraph. You have 4 minutes. (Observe students and give feedback.)

3. (After 4 minutes, say:) Stop writing. I'm going to call on several students to read their sentences about the first picture.
- (Call on several students.)

4. You can figure out things that must have happened in the missing picture by looking at what's different in the last picture. Everything that's different in the last picture gives a clue about what must have happened. Some things in the last picture also give you clues about when something happened.

5. I'll tell about some of the things in the last picture that give big clues about what Jerry or his mother did.
- Touch the sandwich on the table. ✔
  That gives you a clue about something Jerry must have done.
- Touch the wastebasket. ✔
  That gives you another clue about something Jerry must have done.
- Touch the grocery bag in the picture. ✔
  That gives you a clue about where Jerry's mother went. You can see some of the things she bought.

6. Your turn: Write the rest of the paragraph. Write sentences that tell at least five things that must have happened before the last picture. Remember, don't tell about the last picture. Just tell what happened in the missing picture. Raise your hand when you're finished. You have 5 minutes. (Observe students and give feedback.)

7. (After 5 minutes, say:) Stop writing. I'm going to call on several students to read their paragraphs. Listen carefully to each paragraph. Make sure there are sentences that tell about all the important things that must have happened first, next and so forth. Raise your hand if you hear something that's wrong or that's out of the right order.

• (Call on several students to read their paragraphs.)

8. Now you're going to check your paragraph. Make 2 check boxes under your paragraph.

9. Here's check 1: Do your sentences tell what happened first, next and next? Make sure you wrote sentences that tell about five things that must have happened in the missing picture. If you left out a sentence, write the sentence below your paragraph and make an arrow to show where it goes in your paragraph. Make a check in box 1 when you're sure your paragraph tells what happened first, next and next. Raise your hand when you're finished with check 1.

10. Here's check 2: Are all your sentences written correctly? Check for capitals, periods and run-ons. Make sure the sentence that tells what Jerry's mother said is punctuated correctly. Read your paragraph. Fix up any mistakes. Then make a check in box 2. Raise your hand when you're finished.

11. Next time, I'll read some of the **super** paragraphs to you.

74 *Reasoning and Writing, Level C Guide*

Beginning with lesson 71, students write more than one paragraph. The first paragraph is about the first picture; a second paragraph is about the missing picture and the last picture. Here's the student material from lesson 71.

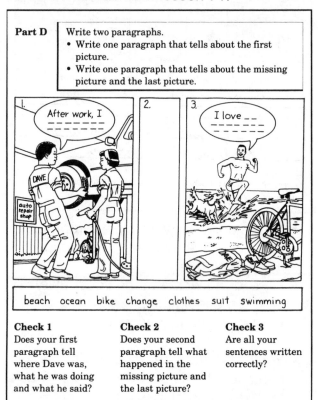

The last main type of inference activity is **setting the scene.** The first activities introduce the idea that descriptions of the scene may tell where characters were and what they **were doing** (rather than what they did). Here's the first part of the exercise from lesson 77.

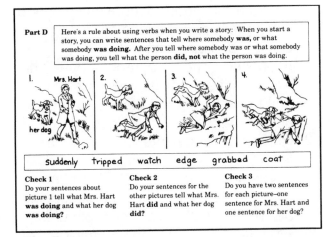

Part D — Here's a rule about using verbs when you write a story: When you start a story, you can write sentences that tell where somebody **was**, or what somebody **was doing**. After you tell where somebody was or what somebody was doing, you tell what the person **did, not** what the person was doing.

1. Mrs. Hart / her dog   2.   3.   4.

suddenly   tripped   watch   edge   grabbed   coat

Check 1
Do your sentences about picture 1 tell what Mrs. Hart **was doing** and what her dog **was doing**?

Check 2
Do your sentences for the other pictures tell what Mrs. Hart **did** and what her dog **did**?

Check 3
Do you have two sentences for each picture—one sentence for Mrs. Hart and one sentence for her dog?

2. Here's a rule about using verbs when you write a story: When you start a story, you can write sentences that tell where somebody **was,** or what somebody **was doing.** After you tell where somebody was or what somebody was doing, you tell what the person **did, not** what the person was doing.

• The pictures show what happened. The first picture shows where Mrs. Hart and her dog were and what they were doing. The other pictures show what happened.

3. You're going to write the first two sentences of your paragraph. You're going to write sentences for the first picture. Write a sentence that tells what Mrs. Hart **was doing.** Then write a sentence that tells what her dog **was doing.** Don't tell what they **did.** Tell what they were doing. Make up sentences that give a clear picture. Raise your hand when you're finished. You have one and a half minutes. (Observe students and give feedback.)

4. (After one and a half minutes, say:) Stop writing. I'm going to call on several students to read their sentences. Listen carefully. One sentence should tell what Mrs. Hart **was doing.** The next sentence should tell what her dog **was doing.**

• (Call on several students to read their sentences. Praise sentences such as: *Mrs. Hart was walking down a hill. Her dog was walking behind her.*)

5. Those sentences tell what Mrs. Hart was doing and what her dog was doing at the beginning of the story. Now things happened. So the rest of your sentences will tell what Mrs. Hart and her dog **did.** They shouldn't tell what they were doing.

• I'll read a good paragraph. Listen: Mrs. Hart was walking down a hill with her dog. Her dog was walking behind her. Suddenly, she tripped over a rock. Her dog stopped and watched her. Mrs. Hart rolled down the hill. Her dog ran after her. Mrs. Hart rolled to the edge of a cliff. Just then, her dog grabbed her by the coat and held onto her.

• Some of the words in that story are in the vocabulary box. I'll read them: suddenly, tripped, watch, edge, grabbed, coat.

6. Listen: Write the rest of the story. For each picture, tell what Mrs. Hart did and what her dog did. Remember, write two sentences for each picture. One sentence should tell about what Mrs. Hart did. The other sentence should tell what her dog did. You can write sentences that begin with a part that tells when. Raise your hand when you're finished. You have 6 minutes. (Observe students and give feedback.)

Clarity

The two main skills emphasized in the clarity activities are **describing the details** that distinguish one thing from similar objects and **using more specific words** instead of general words.

The basic rationale for including specific details is to give the reader a clear picture of the intended event or object.

Here's an early exercise (lesson 28) that requires students to describe specified pictures.

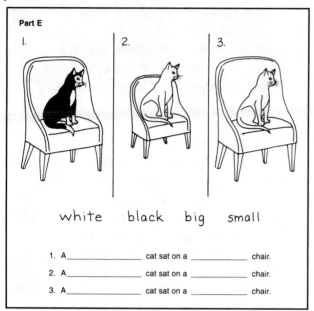

In this exercise, students use adjectives to create sentences that are clear. In similar exercises, students use phrases that tell where someone or something was. (The house had a window on either side of the door.)

Starting in lesson 32, students are introduced to the need for specific, rather than general, words. The clarity exercise presents a paragraph that could generate many possible "pictures" because the words are general. The general words are underlined. Students indicate why each word is too general and then rewrite the paragraph with specific words. Here's the first part of the exercise from lesson 32.

Part D   Rewrite the paragraph so the underlined parts give a clear picture.

An animal fell out of a large old tree. It landed on the soft ground.

A person picked it up. The person put it in a container and took it home.

Here's a rule about good writing: Good writing tells about things so that you can get a clear picture of what happened. The paragraph in part D has words that are unclear because they don't give us a good picture. The unclear words are underlined.

2. I'll read the first sentence: An animal fell out of a large old tree. The unclear words are **an animal.** We don't know what kind of animal to get a picture of. So we could all get different pictures.

• What kind of animal do you think fell out of a large old tree? (**Call on several students. After each suggested animal, say:**) Yes, that's an animal. So that's one of the pictures you could get from the first sentence.

3. Next sentence: It landed on the soft ground. We can get a picture of the soft ground.

4. Next sentence: A person picked it up. The words **a person** are underlined. (**Call on a student:**) Why? (**Praise a response that expresses the idea:** *We don't know what kind of person.*)

• We can get pictures of different persons. I could get a picture of an old man with a long beard.

• What other kind of person could you picture? (**Call on several students. After each suggested person, say:**) Yes, that's a person. So that's one of the pictures you could get from that sentence.

5. Last sentence: The person put it in a container and took it home. You could get pictures of a lot of different persons and a lot of different containers.

• What are some containers the person might have used? (**Call on several students. After each suggested container, say:**) Yes, that's a container. So that's one of the pictures you could get from that sentence.

6. Everybody, take out a sheet of lined paper and write your name on the top line. Raise your hand when you're finished.
- Pencils down. Open your textbook to lesson 32 and find part D.

Part D

| snake | striped | large | wooden | cowgirl |
| wearing | boots | outfit | young | basket |

7. The picture shows what happened. You can see what kind of animal fell out of a tree. You can see the person who picked it up. You can see what kind of container the person put it in.
- You're going to rewrite the paragraph so it lets anybody reading the paragraph get a clear picture of what happened. When you rewrite it, you don't want to call the snake just **a snake.** Call it a **big** snake or **striped** snake.
- You don't want to call the person who picked it up just **a girl.** What could you call that person so somebody could get a clear picture of her? (Call on several students. Ideas: *A young girl; a girl wearing cowgirl clothes.*)
- What are you going to call the container? (Call on several students. Ideas: *A wooden basket.*)

8. I'll read the words in the vocabulary box. Follow along: snake, striped, large, wooden, cowgirl, wearing, boots, outfit, young, basket.
9. Who can say the first sentence with the underlined part changed so it gives a clear picture of the animal? (Call on several students. Praise sentences such as: *A huge striped snake fell out of a large old tree.*)
10. Your turn: Rewrite the paragraph on your lined paper. Remember, change the underlined parts so they give a clear picture. Copy the rest of each sentence. You have 5 minutes. Raise your hand when you're finished. (Observe students and give feedback.)
11. (After 5 minutes, say:) Stop writing. I'm going to call on several students to read their paragraphs. Remember, the only parts of the sentences that should be changed are the underlined parts. The new parts should give a clear picture of what happened. Listen carefully and raise your hand if a sentence is wrong or if it doesn't give a clear picture.
- (Call on several students to read their paragraphs. After each paragraph is read, ask the students:) Does that paragraph give a clear picture? (Praise paragraphs that have clear replacements for the underlined words.)

Following the part of the exercise shown above, students check their work for capitals and periods and judge whether each sentence gives a clear picture of what happened.

In later exercises, students edit paragraphs for unclear parts. They refer to a picture for the specific detail that should be in the paragraph. Here's the student material from lesson 36.

Part C

> They cleaned the animal. She wore great big shoes and dark glasses. She squirted the animal with a hose. He wore a cowboy hat. He sat on the animal and scrubbed its back. She wore a funny suit and a tiny hat. She stood on a ladder. She poured it on the animal.

Part C

In lessons 37 through 82, students continue to edit paragraphs for unclear parts, write descriptions for one of several similar pictures, and apply pronoun clarity rules to sentences that refer to pictures.

In lesson 83, students write a scene-setting description. This activity prepares students for the extended writing assignments that occur later in Level C. Here's the exercise from lesson 83.

Part D

1. Write a description about picture 1. Tell where the girls were and what they were doing.

2. Write a description about picture 2. Tell where the girls were and what they were doing.

- You're going to write descriptions that have more than one sentence. Each description will tell where the girls **were** and what they **were doing.** Each description should give a clear picture.
2. Listen: Your first description will tell about picture 1. Look at picture 1 and make sure you don't say anything that could tell about picture 2.
- Where were the girls in picture 1? (Call on a student. Idea: *On the grass in front of a house.*)
- What were the girls doing in picture 1? (Call on a student. Idea: *Sitting on the grass and reading books.*)
- What kind of house was in picture 1? (Call on a student. Idea: *A large house.*)

3. Write your description for picture 1. Tell where the girls **were** and what they **were doing.** Don't tell what they did. You can write as many sentences as you need. Start your description with **three girls.** First tell where they were. Then tell what they were doing. Raise your hand when you're finished. (Observe students and give feedback.)

4. I'll read a super description for picture 1. Listen: Three girls were in front of a large house. They were sitting on the grass. They were reading books.

5. Let's listen to some of the descriptions you wrote. Listen carefully and make sure the description tells where the girls **were** and what they **were doing.**

   • (Call on several students to read their descriptions. Praise descriptions that tell where the girls were and what they were doing in picture 1.)

6. Now write a description for picture 2. Tell where the girls were and what they were doing. Don't tell what they did. Write as many sentences as you need. You **can't** start your description with three girls because there aren't three girls in that picture. Raise your hand when you're finished with your description.
   (Observe students and give feedback.)

7. I'll read a super description for picture 2. Listen: Two girls were on the grass next to a small house. They were jumping rope.

8. Let's listen to some of the descriptions you wrote. Listen carefully and make sure the description tells where the girls were and what they were doing.

   • (Call on several students to read their descriptions. Praise descriptions that tell where the girls were and what they were doing in picture 2.)

9. Check your descriptions. Make sure the first sentence tells where the girls were. Make sure the second description tells what the girls were doing.

Teaching Notes

Students are to write sentences that use the verb **were.** Reinforce students who write descriptions that may sound a little mechanical. Each sentence of the model in step 4 presents only one detail. (They were sitting on the grass. They were reading books.) These sentences are quite acceptable. Sentences such as, "They were sitting on the grass, reading books," are not necessarily preferable for students who are learning to write. In fact, these sentences may involve punctuation conventions students haven't yet learned. If students write sentences that combine details, simply say, "Yes, you can write it that way." But don't present the sentence to the group as something others should try to imitate.

Like the other skills that are taught in Level C, clarity becomes an important tool for students to use when evaluating their writing. They can't evaluate sentences or passages for "clarity" unless they have learned skills. The skills are taught in Level C, starting with a simple context and moving progressively to the context of student writing where the skills will be used for as long as students write.

Expanded Writing Process

The expanded writing process begins in lesson 91 and continues to the end of the program. These activities expand what students have learned about drawing inferences, paragraphing and rewriting passages. Typically, students work on a particular story for two lessons. For some assignments, students write endings to stories that you read. For other assignments, students infer what must have happened before the events shown in an illustration.

Here's an exercise from lesson 95. Students tell about the events that occurred before the picture, describe the problem the man had in the picture, and tell how the man solved his problem.

Part C

Here's how to write interesting stories:
1. **Tell about the characters at the beginning of the story.**
   Tell where they were.
   Describe them and name them.
2. **Tell about their problem.**
   Tell what they wanted to do and why they couldn't do it.
3. **Tell the things they did to solve their problem.**
4. **Tell how the story ends.**
   Tell whether they solved their problem.

Write an interesting story.

embarrassed   money   wallet   suddenly   blushed   glared

- I'll read what it says. Follow along. Here's how to write interesting stories:
  1. **Tell about the characters at the beginning of the story.** Tell where they were. Describe them and name them.
  2. **Tell about their problem.** Tell what they wanted to do and why they couldn't do it.
  3. **Tell the things they did to solve their problem.**
  4. **Tell how the story ends.** Tell whether they solved their problem.
2. Remember those steps. First tell where the characters were at the beginning of the story. Then tell about their problem. Then tell what they did to solve their problem. Then tell how the story ends. Tell whether they solved their problem.

3. Look at the picture. You're going to write a **whole story** about this picture.
- The man doesn't have a name. The man in the picture has a serious problem.
- What does he want to do? (Call on a student. Idea: *Pay for his meal.*)
- Part of his problem is that he wants to pay for his lunch. Why doesn't he just reach in his pocket and pull out the money to pay for his lunch? (Call on a student. Idea: *He doesn't have any money in his pocket.*)
- That's the other part of his problem. He wants to pay for his lunch, but he lost his money or forgot his wallet. Everybody, do you think he knew he didn't have his money before he got to the cash register? (Signal.) *No.*
- He was embarrassed. He blushed. He felt stupid. How did that woman feel? (Call on a student. Idea: *Angry.*)
4. When you write the first part of your story, you'll describe the man and tell his name. Then you'll tell where he was and what he did before he discovered that he had a problem.
- The sign on the window says **Rosy's Cafe.** That's where he ate. You could tell what he ate. You'll have to make that up. Then tell how he discovered that he had a problem and how he felt.
5. Your turn: Write the first part of your story. You can write as many paragraphs as you want for the first part. For this story, you can tell the things that people said and how they felt. **Don't tell what the man did to solve the problem.** Just tell about the problem. Raise your hand when you're finished. You have 7 minutes.
(Observe students and give feedback.)

6. (After 7 minutes, say:) Stop writing. Check the first part of your story.

- Raise your hand if you gave the man a name.
  Hands down.
- Raise your hand if you described how the man looked.
  Hands down.
- Raise your hand if you told where the man was and what he did before he discovered his problem.
  Hands down.
- Raise your hand if you told what the man's problem was.
  Hands down.
- Raise your hand if you told where he was when he discovered that he didn't have any money.
  Hands down.
- Raise your hand if you told how he felt when he discovered that he didn't have any money.
  Hands down.

7. If you told all those things, you have a great beginning for your story. But to make it a story, you have to tell how the man solved his problem. That man can't just say, "I'll bring you the money later."

- Why not? (Call on a student. Idea: *The woman wouldn't accept that solution.*)
- Think of some of the things the woman might agree to. Tell what the man said and what the woman said. Then tell everything the man did to solve his problem. You can tell how he felt at the end of the story.
- Everybody, do you think that man will ever make that kind of mistake again? (Signal.) *No.*

8. Write the rest of the story. Make it interesting. Remember, tell the things the characters did and said. Give a clear picture. Raise your hand when you're finished. You have 15 minutes. (Observe students and give feedback.)

9. (After 15 minutes, say:) Stop writing. Check the last part of your story.

- Raise your hand if you told some things the man said to the woman.
  Hands down.
- Raise your hand if you told some things the woman said to the man.
  Hands down.
- Raise your hand if you told what the man did after the woman agreed to a plan.
  Hands down.
- If you told all those things, you told how the man solved the problem.

10. I'll mark your papers before the next lesson and tell you about any mistakes. You'll have a chance to rewrite your story then.

Teaching Notes

Students have some latitude about making up details to fill in the story. Praise accounts that are reasonable. Discourage accounts that provide too much information about what he ate and other details that are not necessary to set the scene.

In lesson 96, students work in teams to revise and rewrite their story. Here's the exercise.

These are questions about the story you wrote. If the answer to all nine questions is **yes,** you wrote a super story. If any answer is **no,** you'll fix up the story so the answer is **yes.** Then you'll have a super story.

2. I'll read the questions about the problem:
   1. Did you give the man a name?
   2. Did you describe the man?
   3. Did you tell where he was and what he did before he discovered that he had a problem?
   4. Did you tell what the man's problem was?
   5. Did you tell where he was when he discovered that he had a problem?
   6. Did you tell how he felt when he discovered that he had a problem?
3. I'll read the questions about the rest of the story:
   7. Did you tell some things the man said to the woman?
   8. Did you tell some things the woman said to the man?
   9. Did you tell what the man did after the woman agreed to a plan?
4. Write the numbers 1 through 9 at the top of the story you wrote.
   • Read your story over and figure out the things your story did **not** tell. Circle the number of each question your story did not answer. Remember, if your story does not tell about something, circle the number of the question at the top of your story. Do it now. Raise your hand when you're finished.
   (Observe students and give feedback.)
5. I'll read a super story. This story answers all nine questions. Listen:

Tim Carson was at Rosy's Cafe. Tim was a chubby man who had lost most of his hair. He was wearing a shirt and a tie. Tim had a hamburger, some fries and a glass of milk. The bill was two dollars and fifty cents. Tim walked up to the counter and was ready to pay for his lunch. He reached into his pocket for his wallet. Suddenly, he blushed. He didn't have his wallet. He didn't have any money at all. Rosy leaned over the counter and glared at him. He didn't know what to do. He was very embarrassed.

At last, he said, "I don't have any money with me. I can bring the money by later."

Rosy looked at him and said, "Wrong."

He said, "But Rosy, I work in the bank on the next block. You can trust me."

Rosy said, "Wrong."

Suddenly, Tim got an idea. He said, "I'll leave my watch here. It's worth over 50 dollars. Then I'll go get the money and bring it right back."

Rosy looked at the watch. Finally, she said, "All right." Then she said, "But if you don't come back, I'll keep the watch."

Tim agreed. He went back to the bank and looked for his wallet. It was in his jacket pocket. He grabbed the wallet, ran back to Rosy's Cafe, paid for his lunch, took his watch and ran back to the bank. He got back late. His boss glared at him. Tim blushed again and said to himself, "I'll never make that mistake again."

6. Now you're going to work in teams to figure out how you can make your stories better. The team members will take turns reading their stories. After a student reads, that student will have the first turn to tell what would make the story better. Then the other members of the team can give suggestions to make the story better. Remember, these suggestions shouldn't change what happens in the story. They should just make the story better so it answers all the questions. The team should agree on all changes.

7. (Assign the first student in each team to read.) Raise your hand when your team has finished talking about the first student's story.
   (Observe teams. Praise teams that are working cooperatively.)

8. (For each team with hands raised, ask about the suggestions for the first student's story; praise good suggestions; then tell the second team member to read his or her story.)

   • Raise your hand when your team has finished talking about the second student's story.
     (Observe teams. Praise teams that are working cooperatively.)

9. (Repeat step 8 until all students have received feedback on their story.)

10. Now you'll rewrite your story. Start with the story you wrote earlier. Cross out any sentences or parts that you want to change. Then start with a fresh sheet of paper and rewrite your story. Copy any parts that you want to keep. Try to put in all the suggestions that will make your story better. Also, look at any mistakes I marked on the story you wrote last time. Make sure your rewritten story doesn't have any of those mistakes. Also, make sure you have at least three sentences that begin with a part that tells when. Raise your hand when you're finished. You have 20 minutes.
    (Observe students and give feedback.)

11. (After 20 minutes, say:) Stop writing. If you didn't finish rewriting your story, you can finish it later. Then you'll check your story.
    (Direct students either to check story on their own or in teams.)

    • When you check your story, fix it up if there's a problem. Make sure that it's a finished story that you'll be proud of. Take the time you need to make it really good. You don't have to hand it in until (specify time), but if you finish it earlier, you can hand it in earlier.

12. Here are the checks for your story:
    • Check 1: Does your story answer all nine questions?
    • Check 2: Did you write at least three sentences that begin with a part that tells when?
    • Check 3: Are all your sentences punctuated correctly?

13. At the beginning of the next period, I'll read some of the **super** stories.

Teaching Notes

In steps 7 through 9, students work in teams. The simplest way to assure that students work well in teams is to make comments about teams that are working well. "Wow, I've just heard some good suggestions from this team. They are working well."

If students are passive, offer a reinforcer. For example, "All students who write a much better story than the first time will receive ten bonus points. So work hard in your teams. Make sure all your members know how to make their story better."

The final expanded writing process involves topics and letters. One of the topics students write on is, "Why do I like summertime the best?" Later, they write on the topic, "Why do I like wintertime the best?" This introduction to persuasive writing sets the stage for the work on analyzing arguments that they will do in Level D.

Teaching Notes

Throughout the program, students follow different instructions on different lessons. If you make sure early in the program that students are following directions carefully, they will perform much better near the end of the program, where students are to follow elaborate directions. These directions are usually a chain of things students have done before. The students who are practiced in following the component directions will learn a lot about writing.

The expanded writing process is designed to teach students important concepts and practices. Students learn what main idea is because they construct main-idea sentences and use them as foundations for passages. Students learn to discriminate between trivial and relevant detail because they perform many inferences that require identification of the relevant details and differences between two pictures. The most difficult practice students learn is to check their writing for multiple criteria. The expanded writing process gives students repeated practice in applying all editing skills they have learned.

Tests

In—program Tests

The in-program tests that appear as every tenth lesson of the program provide a basis for periodically judging the progress of individual students and for awarding grades.

During a test, students should be seated so that they cannot "copy."

Directions for presenting the test appear as part of each test lesson.

The answer key for each test appears in the Answer Key book. When observing students' performance, make sure that they are following directions, but do not tell them answers to any item or give them hints.

Mark each item a student misses on the test.

Count the number of mistakes and enter the number at the top of each student's test. If the student missed three items, the score is 3.

Before returning the test forms, use your copy of the Reproducible Group Summary Sheets (pages 97 and 98) and enter the number of errors each student made.

Reasoning and Writing, Level C has ten in—program tests. Tests 6 and 9 are paragraph—writing tests. An optional reproducible summary for Test 6 and 9 appears on page 99.

Test Remedies

Test remedies are specified as part of each test lesson (under the heading **Test Remedies**). The criterion for determining whether or not students need a remedy is the percentage of students that make mistakes on a particular part of the test. The criteria are specified as part of the test lesson. Typically, the criteria are stated like this:

If more than 1/4 of the students make 2 or more errors in part ___, present the following exercises. (A list follows.)

The remedies indicate what you should do if the class has problems; however, the guidelines for providing remedies are quite general. Here are more specific guidelines.

1. If students perform poorly on a test, they will probably have trouble on later exercises in the program and should be given a remedy before the next lesson is presented.

2. In many classrooms, the same students tend to perform poorly on different tests; if those are the only students who perform poorly, do not present the remedy to the entire class. If possible, present the remedy only to the students who need it.

3. If it's not possible to schedule a time for providing the remedy to a small group of students (and not the entire class) give the students who performed well a writing assignment similar to the ones on the lessons preceding the test. As they work on the assignment, present the remedies to the students who need additional help.

4. If more than one-fourth of the students have trouble with a part of the test, present the remedy for that part to all students. Then present the lesson following the test.

5. If more than one-fourth of students repeatedly make an unacceptably high number of errors on the tests, try to analyze what's wrong. Possibly, the students should not be placed in Level C. Possibly, they are not trying very hard.

6. Use effective enforcement practices to prompt harder work and better performance. A good guide is *The Solution Book* by Randall Sprick. This text, published by SRA, contains specific suggestions for increasing student motivation.

Objectives

The objectives show the development of skills and operations taught in *Reasoning and Writing, Level C.*

The skills and operations are grouped by tracks. The headings indicate the major tracks and the divisions within each track. Each track shows the development of a major topic, such as sentence analysis or mechanics. Typically, a track will have activities that are presented over many different lessons of the program.

The major tracks are:

DEDUCTIONS
SENTENCE ANALYSIS
MECHANICS
EDITING
REPORTING—BASED ON PICTURES
INFERRING—BASED ON PICTURES
CLARITY—BASED ON PICTURES
RELEVANCE
EXPANDED WRITING PROCESS

Within each track are divisions. Each division is marked by a subheading.

The subheadings for Sentence Analysis are:

SUBJECT-PREDICATE
VERBS
PRONOUNS
NOUNS
ADJECTIVES
CONSOLIDATION

The subheadings for Mechanics are:

GENERAL
CAPITALS AND ENDING MARKS
APOSTROPHES
QUOTES
COMMAS

Although the objectives show the various categories and the lessons in which each specific objective is taught, the objectives do not show the interrelationships among the various skills. Specific skills are involved in more than one track. For instance, students learn to write and punctuate sentences that begin with a part that tells when (*After Ted left the meeting, he met Mary*). This particular sentence type is analyzed and used in the following tracks: Sentence Analysis, Editing, Mechanics and Reporting—Based on Pictures. Students also write sentences of this type in Expanded Writing Process assignments.

Similarly, identifying subjects and predicates of sentences is a foundation skill that is developed in the Sentence Analysis track, but also appears in the Mechanics track and in the Editing track. When students edit passages for capitals and periods, they must first identify the sentences. They use the subject-predicate analysis for this identification. Subject-predicate analysis is also used in the instruction for parts of speech, especially pronouns.

In summary, the objectives show the various skills and operations that are taught; however, skills and operations developed in one track invariably spill over into other tracks as students use and apply what they have learned.

	OBJECTIVES	LESSONS
Deductions	Complete a simple deduction.	1–3
	Draw conclusions based on different concrete examples.	4–6, 8, 12

Sentence Analysis

	OBJECTIVES	LESSONS
Subject-Predicate	Identify the part of a sentence that names.	1–3
	Identify the part of a sentence that names (subject) and the part that tells more (predicate).	4–9, 19
	Indicate the subject of sentences in a paragraph.	11–16
	Indicate the subject and predicate of sentences.	21–24, 27, 28, 31
	Construct sentences by combining specific subjects and predicates.	25, 26, 32, 37
	Identify sentence parts as subjects or predicates.	33–35
	Identify the subject, predicate and verb in sentences.	41–43
	Indicate the part of predicates that tells when.	58–61
	Identify subject, predicate and part that tells when in sentence pairs.	62, 63
	Rewrite sentences so they begin with the part of the predicate that tells when.	65–68
	Rewrite a paragraph so some sentences begin with the part of the predicate that tells when.	73, 80
	Complete sentences that begin with a 1-word or 2-word part that tells when.	76
	Discriminate sentences from sentence fragments.	105, 106, 109
Verbs	Change regular present-time verbs to past-time verbs by adding the suffix **e-d.**	4
	Write past-time verbs for irregular present-time verbs.	5, 6, 8, 11–14, 21–23, 25–29, 35–38, 42
	Change 2-word verbs in sentences to 1-word verbs.	6–9, 11, 13–16
	Change 2-word verbs in a paragraph to 1-word past-time verbs.	18, 19, 22
	Identify the verbs in sentences.	40, 53, 57
	Identify 2-word verbs.	44
	Identify the two actions specified in a sentence.	45
	Discriminate between run-on sentences and sentences that name two actions.	46, 47

	OBJECTIVES	LESSONS
	Identify the verbs in sentences that have 1-word verbs and in sentences that have 2-word verbs.	45–48
	Identify the verbs presented in a group of words.	51, 52, 54
	Select the appropriate verb (**was** or **were**) to agree with the subject of the sentence.	81–84
Pronouns	Replace the subject of a sentence with the appropriate pronoun (**he, she, it** or **they**).	7–9, 11–13 32–34, 54
	Use appropriate pronouns in a short passage.	14–17, 24
	Use appropriate pronouns (**he, she** or **it**) in a paragraph.	25–29
	Determine whether it is appropriate to use a pronoun as the subject of a sentence.	41–43, 51–54
	Determine whether the subject of a sentence is a pronoun.	55
	Change sentences with noun subjects into sentences with pronoun subjects.	56, 57
	Determine whether it is appropriate to use a pronoun (**him** or **her**) in the predicate of a sentence.	58, 59
	For sentence pairs, indicate whether the noun or the pronoun (**they** or **them**) is appropriate in the second sentence.	63, 64
	Match nouns with appropriate pronoun referents.	65, 66
	Match pronouns (**I, me, we, us**) with appropriate referents.	87, 88
Nouns	Identify the noun in the subject of a sentence.	63–65
	Determine whether isolated words are nouns.	71, 72
	Identify nouns in the subject and predicate of sentences.	73
Adjectives	Identify the noun and each adjective in sentence subjects.	91–93
	Identify nouns and adjectives in sentences.	94, 95, 97, 98
	Complete a subject by writing adjectives in front of given nouns.	96
Consolidation	Identify pronouns and verbs in sentences.	58, 59, 61, 63, 64, 67
	Identify nouns and pronouns in sentence subjects.	66, 67
	Identify nouns, pronouns and verbs in sentences.	68, 69, 72, 74–76
	Identify the subject and predicate of sentences and indicate the part of speech of specific words.	77, 78, 81, 82, 86, 87, 89–91, 96, 99, 101–105, 107, 109, 110

Mechanics	OBJECTIVES	LESSONS
General	Follow conventions for using lined paper (numbers with periods before the margin, sentences with capitals and periods after the margin).	1, 2
	Copy item numbers and sentences onto lined paper.	3
	Copy a paragraph.	15–18
Capitals and Ending Marks	Punctuate sentences (capitals and periods) and identify the subject of the sentences in a paragraph.	17–19, 21–23
	Punctuate sentences (capitals and periods) in a paragraph.	24–26, 28, 29, 31, 32
	Capitalize the name of a person.	29
	Capitalize all parts of a person's name.	31–34
	Capitalize people's names in a paragraph.	35
	Identify and punctuate sentences that ask a question.	68, 69
	Complete sentences with the word **said** or **asked** and the appropriate ending mark.	71–73
	Apply capitalization rules for names of people, days of the week and months of the year.	85, 86
	Apply capitalization rules for names of persons or places.	97–99
Apostrophes	Rewrite expressions so that a word is written with an apostrophe **(the dress that belongs to the girl** becomes **the girl's dress).**	44, 45
	Construct sentences with possessive words, for example: **girl's.**	46–48
	Complete sentences with possessive words in the predicate, for example: **A mouse sat on Milly's foot.**	49, 51
	Discriminate between plural nouns and possessive nouns.	52, 53
Quotes	Punctuate sentences with quotations, for example: **John said, "I'm tired."**	53–58
	Punctuate statements and questions with quotations.	59, 60
	Punctuate two-sentence quotations, for example: **Joe said, "I'm hot. Let's go swimming."**	65, 66
Commas	Punctuate sentences that begin with the part that tells when.	64
	Identify and punctuate sentences that begin with the part that tells when.	69, 71
	Punctuate sentences that have a series of noun or verb phrases.	77–79, 81
	Rewrite sentences that have a series of noun or verb phrases.	82, 83

Editing

OBJECTIVES	LESSONS
Edit sentences for irregular past-time verbs.	30, 31, 33
Edit a paragraph for capitals, periods and past-time verbs.	33, 34, 39
Edit a paragraph for **he, she, it** and **they.**	35
Edit a paragraph for sentences that begin with **and** or **and then.**	36, 37, 38
Edit a paragraph to correct unclear parts.	36, 37, 39
Edit a paragraph for periods and capitals, including people's names.	37, 41
Edit run-on sentences.	39–41
Edit a paragraph for run-on sentences.	42–45, 58
Edit sentences for multiple criteria (verb agreement, apostrophes, run-ons, capitals, commas, quotes and sentence fragments).	55, 56, 62, 64, 67, 68, 74, 75, 79, 83, 88, 89, 94, 104, 108, 110

Reporting—Based on Pictures

Discriminate between sentences that report on a picture versus sentences that convey an inference.	1–4, 6, 7
Write appropriate subjects in sentences.	1–3
Construct sentences by combining given parts that name and parts that tell more.	4, 5
Select sentences that state the main thing that illustrated characters did.	6–8
Construct sentences that state the main thing that illustrated characters did.	9, 11–16
Select the appropriate name for a group.	15, 16
Select sentences that state the main thing that illustrated groups did.	17–19
Construct a paragraph that reports on what the members of an illustrated group did.	19–23
Write a sentence that states the main thing an illustrated group did.	21–24
Write two sentences about an illustrated character.	26, 27
Construct a paragraph that includes one sentence about an illustrated group and two sentences about each illustrated character.	28, 29, 31, 41
Write a paragraph that reports on an illustrated action sequence.	36–39

OBJECTIVES	LESSONS
Write a short paragraph that includes a sentence that has a direct quote.	61, 62
Construct sentences that begin with the part of the predicate that tells when.	69, 70, 72, 75
Write sentences that have a series of noun phrases.	85, 86, 90
Write sentences that have a series of verb phrases.	87–89

Inferring—Based on Pictures

Write a paragraph that infers what must have happened in a missing picture.	47–50
Write a paragraph that infers what must have happened in a missing picture and that reports on the last picture.	51–59
Write a paragraph that indicates the chronology of important events implied by two pictures.	61, 62
Write a paragraph that a) infers the chronology of important events and b) includes a direct 1-sentence quote.	63–66, 69
Write a paragraph that a) infers the chronology of important events and b) includes a direct 2-sentence quote.	67, 68
Write a 2-paragraph story that infers and reports.	71–76
Write a paragraph in which progressive verbs are used to set the scene.	77–79, 81
Write a 2-paragraph passage that first sets the scene and then tells what the characters did.	82, 83
Write a 3-paragraph story that first sets the scene and then tells what the characters did.	84–86
Apply the rule that only one person can talk in a paragraph.	87–89

Clarity—Based on Pictures

Identify the set of pictures a sentence describes.	11–14, 17
Identify sentences that tell about all of the pictures, two of the pictures and one of the pictures.	23–25, 27
Complete similar sentences so they tell about only one picture.	28–31
Rewrite a paragraph to correct unclear parts.	32–35
Write a sentence that tells about only one of two similar pictures.	34, 35
Write a sentence that tells about only one of three similar pictures.	38, 39

OBJECTIVES	LESSONS
Write a paragraph that tells about one of two similar pictures.	42–49
Write two sentences that tell about one of two similar pictures.	43–45
Apply pronoun **(he** or **she)** clarity rules to complete sentences that refer to a picture.	55–57
Identify sets of pictures that are consistent with different descriptions.	76–80
Write a 2-sentence description that tells about only one of four similar pictures.	81, 82
Write a scene-setting description for one of two similar pictures.	83, 84

Relevance

Determine whether facts are relevant to a question.	34–36, 38, 39, 92
Indicate whether sentences in a passage are relevant to a given topic.	93–95, 97
Construct a sentence from a question and an answer.	101–103
Write title sentences for short passages.	106–108

Expanded Writing Process

Write a multiparagraph ending for a story.	91, 93
Revise and rewrite a multiparagraph ending.	92
Write a multiparagraph story.	95, 97, 99
Revise, rewrite and check a multiparagraph story.	96, 98, 100
Write a passage about a specified topic.	101, 103, 110
Revise, rewrite and check a passage on a specified topic.	102, 104
Write a letter that describes an adventure.	105
Revise, rewrite and check a letter that describes an adventure.	106
Write a letter to complain about a product.	107, 109
Revise, rewrite and check a letter that complains about a product.	108

Skills Profile — Page 1   Name _____

The charts on pages 93 to 96 may be reproduced to make a skills profile for each student. The charts summarize the skills presented in *Reasoning and Writing C* and provide space for indicating the date on which the student completes the lessons in which the skills are taught.

Grade or year in school _____

Teacher's name _____

Starting lesson _____ Date _____

Last lesson completed _____ Date _____ Number of days absent ____

Skills	Taught in These Lessons	Date Lessons Completed	Skills	Taught in These Lessons	Date Lessons Completed
DEDUCTIONS			Discriminates sentences from sentence fragments	105–109	
Completes a simple deduction	1–3				
Draws conclusions based on different concrete examples	4–12		**Verbs**		
			Changes regular present-time verbs to past-time verbs by adding **e-d**	4	
SENTENCE ANALYSIS					
Subject-Predicate					
Identifies the part of a sentence that names (subject) and the part that tells more (predicate)	1–31		Writes past-time verbs for irregular present-time verbs	5–42	
			Changes 2-word verbs in sentences to 1-word verbs	6–16	
Indicates the subjects of sentences in a paragraph	11–16		Changes 2-word verbs in a paragraph to 1-word past-time verbs	18–22	
Constructs sentences by combining specific subjects and predicates	25–37				
Identifies sentence parts as subjects or predicates	33–35		Identifies the verbs in sentences	40–57	
Identifies the subjects, predicates and verbs in sentences	41–43		Discriminates between run-on sentences and sentences that name two actions	46–47	
Indicates the parts of predicates that tell when	58–61		Identifies the verbs in sentences that have 1-word verbs and in sentences that have 2-word verbs	45–48	
Identifies the subjects, predicates and parts that tell when in sentence pairs	62–63		Identifies the verbs presented in a group of words	51–54	
Rewrites sentences so they begin with the part of the predicate that tells when	65–68		Selects the appropriate verb (**was** or **were**) to agree with the subject of the sentence	81–84	
Rewrites a paragraph so some sentences begin with the part of the predicate that tells when	73–80		**Pronouns**		
			Replaces the subject of a sentence with the appropriate pronoun (**he, she, it** or **they**)	7–54	

Skills	Taught in These Lessons	Date Lessons Completed	Skills	Taught in These Lessons	Date Lessons Completed
Uses appropriate pronouns in a short passage or paragraph	14–29		Identifies the subjects and predicates of sentences and indicates the parts of speech of specific words	77–110	
Determines whether it is appropriate to use a pronoun as the subject of a sentence	41–58		**MECHANICS** **General** Follows conventions for using lined paper	1–3	
Determines whether the subject of a sentence is a pronoun	55		Copies a paragraph	15–18	
Changes sentences with noun subjects into sentences with pronoun subjects	56–57		**Capitals and Ending Marks** Punctuates sentences (capitals and periods) and identifies the subjects of the sentences in a paragraph	17–23	
Determines whether it is appropriate to use a pronoun (**him** or **her**) in the predicate of a sentence	58–59		Punctuates sentences (capitals and periods) in a paragraph	24–32	
For sentence pairs, indicates whether the noun or the pronoun (**they** or **them**) is appropriate in the second sentence	63–64		Capitalizes all parts of a person's name	29–35	
Matches nouns with appropriate pronoun referents	65–66		Identifies and punctuates sentences that ask a question	68–69	
Matches pronouns (**I, me, we, us**) with appropriate referents	87–88		Completes sentences with the word **said** or **asked** and the appropriate ending mark	71–73	
Nouns Identifies the nouns in the subjects of sentences	63–65		Applies capitalization rules for names of people, days of the week and months of the year	85–86	
Determines whether isolated words are nouns	71–72		Applies capitalization rules for names of persons or places	97–99	
Identifies nouns in the subjects and predicates of sentences	73		**Apostrophes** Rewrites expressions so that a word is written with an apostrophe	44–45	
Adjectives Identifies nouns and adjectives in sentences	91–98		Constructs sentences with possessive words	46–48	
Completes a subject by writing adjectives in front of given nouns	96		Completes sentences with possessive words in the predicate	49–51	
Consolidation Identifies pronouns and verbs in sentences	58–67		Discriminates between plural nouns and possessive nouns	52–53	
Identifies nouns and pronouns in sentence subjects	66–67		**Quotes** Punctuates statements and questions with quotations	53–60	
Identifies nouns, pronouns and verbs in sentences	68–76		Punctuates two-sentence quotations	65–66	

Skills Profile — Page 3 Name _____

Skills	Taught in These Lessons	Date Lessons Completed
Commas		
Punctuates sentences that begin with the part that tells when	64	
Identifies and punctuates sentences that begin with the part that tells when	69–71	
Punctuates sentences that have a series of noun or verb phrases	77–81	
Rewrites sentences that have a series of noun or verb phrases	82–83	
EDITING		
Edits sentences for irregular past-time verbs	30–33	
Edits a paragraph for capitals, periods and past-time verbs	33–41	
Edits a paragraph for **he, she, it** and **they**	35	
Edits a paragraph for sentences that begin with **and** or **and then**	36–38	
Edits a paragraph to correct unclear parts	36–39	
Edits run-on sentences	39–58	
Edits sentences for multiple criteria (verb agreement, apostrophes, run-ons, capitals, commas, quotes and sentence fragments)	55–110	
REPORTING—BASED ON PICTURES		
Discriminates between sentences that report on a picture versus sentences that convey an inference	1–7	
Writes appropriate subjects in sentences	1–3	
Constructs sentences by combining given parts that name and parts that tell more	4–5	
Selects sentences that state the main thing that illustrated characters did	6–8	

Skills	Taught in These Lessons	Date Lessons Completed
Constructs sentences that state the main thing that illustrated characters did	9–16	
Selects the appropriate name for a group	15–16	
Selects sentences that state the main thing that illustrated groups did	17–19	
Constructs a paragraph that reports on what the members of an illustrated group did	19–23	
Writes a sentence that states the main thing an illustrated group did	21–24	
Writes two sentences about an illustrated character	26–27	
Constructs a paragraph that includes one sentence about an illustrated group and two sentences about each illustrated character	28–41	
Writes a paragraph that reports on an illustrated action sequence	36–39	
Writes a short paragraph that includes a sentence that has a direct quote	61–62	
Constructs sentences that begin with the part of the predicate that tells when	69-75	
Writes sentences that have a series of noun or verb phrases	85–90	
INFERRING—BASED ON PICTURES		
Writes a paragraph that infers what must have happened in a missing picture	47–50	
Writes a paragraph that infers what must have happened in a missing picture and that reports on the last picture	51–59	
Writes a paragraph that indicates the chronology of important events implied by two pictures	61–62	

Skills	Taught in These Lessons	Date Lessons Completed	Skills	Taught in These Lessons	Date Lessons Completed
Writes a paragraph that infers the chronology of important events and includes direct quotes	63–69		Applies pronoun (**he** or **she**) clarity rules to complete sentences that refer to a picture	55–57	
Writes a 2-paragraph story that infers and reports	71–76		Identifies sets of pictures that are consistent with different descriptions	76–80	
Writes a paragraph in which progressive verbs are used to set the scene	77–81		Writes a 2-sentence description that tells about only one of four similar pictures	81–82	
Writes a multiparagraph passage that first sets the scene and then tells what the characters did	82–86		Writes a scene-setting description for one of two similar pictures	83–84	
Applies the rule that only one person can talk in a paragraph	87–89		**RELEVANCE**		
CLARITY—BASED ON PICTURES			Determines whether facts are relevant to a question	34–92	
Identifies the set of pictures a sentence describes	11–17		Indicates whether sentences in a passage are relevant to a given topic	93–97	
Identifies sentences that tell about all of the pictures, two of the pictures and one of the pictures	23–27		Constructs a sentence from a question and an answer	101–103	
Completes similar sentences so they tell about only one picture	28–31		Writes title sentences for short passages	106–108	
Rewrites a paragraph to correct unclear parts	32–35		**EXPANDED WRITING PROCESS**		
Writes sentences that tell about only one of two or three similar pictures	34–45		Writes, revises and rewrites a multiparagraph story or ending for a story	91–100	
Writes a paragraph that tells about one of two similar pictures	42–49		Writes, revises, rewrites and checks a passage on a specified topic	101–110	
			Writes, revises, rewrites and checks a letter	105–109	

Summary Sheet

Names	Test 1					Test 2					Test 3					Test 4					Test 5				
	A	B	C	D	Total	A	B	C	D	Total	A	B	C	D	Total	A	B	C	D	Total	A	B	C	D	Total

Summary Sheet

Names	Test 6 Paragraph Total	Test 7					Test 8					Test 9 Paragraph Total	Test 10				
		A	B	C	D	Total	A	B	C	D	Total		A	B	C	D	Total

Optional Summary for Paragraph-Writing Tests

Test 6   ## Test 9

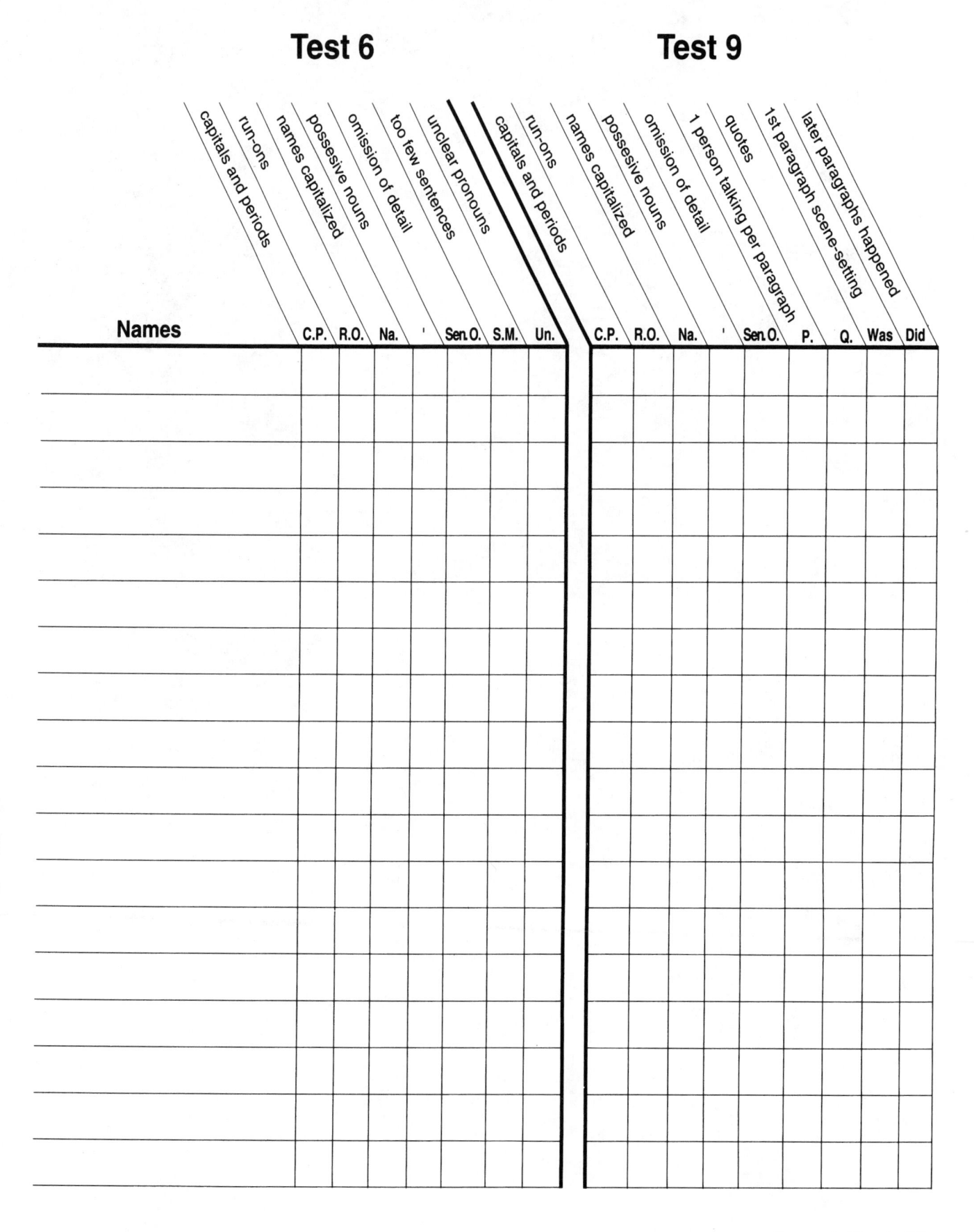

Names	C.P.	R.O.	Na.	'	Sen.O.	S.M.	Un.	C.P.	R.O.	Na.	'	Sen.O.	P.	Q.	Was	Did

Column headers Test 6: capitals and periods, run-ons, names capitalized, possesive nouns, omission of detail, too few sentences, unclear pronouns

Column headers Test 9: capitals and periods, run-ons, names capitalized, possesive nouns, omission of detail, 1 person talking per paragraph, quotes, 1st paragraph scene-setting, later paragraphs happened